D0906515

Careers in Focus

MATHEMATICS
AND PHYSICS

SECOND EDITION

Ferguson
An imprint of Infobase Publishing

Careers in Focus: Mathematics and Physics, Second Edition

Copyright © 2008 by Infobase Publishing

Ferguson
An imprint of Infobase Publishing
132 West 31st Street
New York NY 10001

Library of Congress Cataloging-in-Publication Data

Careers in focus. Mathematics and physics. — 2nd ed.
    p. cm.
Includes bibliographical references and index.
ISBN-13: 978-0-8160-7274-3
ISBN-10: 0-8160-7274-4
1. Mathematics—Vocational guidance. 2. Physics—Vocational guidance. I. Title: Mathematics and physics.
QA10.5.C37 2008
510.23—dc22
                              2007037785

Ferguson books are available at special discounts when purchased in bulk quantities for businesses, associations, institutions, or sales promotions. Please call our Special Sales Department in New York at (212) 967-8800 or (800) 322-8755.

You can find Ferguson on the World Wide Web at http://www.fergpubco.com

Text design by David Strelecky
Cover design by Salvatore Luongo

Printed in the United States of America

MP MSRF 10 9 8 7 6 5 4 3 2

Table of Contents

Introduction

Mathematics and physics are closely related natural sciences. Mathematics is the science and study of numbers and how they relate with each other. Physics is the study of the basic elements and laws of the universe.

Since the 1800s, the fields of mathematics and physics have grown so much that each profession has its own specialized workers. Yet the lines between the two fields, and even among these and other sciences, are not as clear as they used to be. Professionals in these fields orbit the earth, help cure disease, develop fuels for energy and warmth, and even contribute to our understanding of skateboarding, karate, and the sound systems at concerts.

Because the two fields are related, physicists and mathematicians work in many of the same areas. Many ideas and developments in physics, chemistry, the biological sciences, astronomy, and even social sciences (like economics and psychology) rely on ideas from mathematics. These scientific fields offer many careers, including in such areas as astronomy; space technology; energy and resources; earth, ocean, and space science; electronics; industry; computer science; medicine; communications; environmental science; and consulting. Mathematicians and physicists work as engineers, teachers, researchers, lab technicians and supervisors, acoustical scientists, astronomers, astrophysicists, medical physicists, and geophysicists, as well as in other positions. Knowledge in math or physics opens opportunities even for writers, lawyers, and administrators.

Employment opportunities also exist worldwide in government, industry, schools, and private organizations. For instance, mathematicians such as statisticians, operations researchers, and actuaries work in such government agencies as the Department of Health and Human Services, the Government Accountability Office, and the Office of Management and Budget. They help gather information on how many people are likely to get cancer from smoking. They help the president understand how much money our country has and owes other countries. They even help figure out how tax laws can benefit certain people. Other government agencies that employ mathematicians and physicists include the Department of Energy, the Department of Defense, the National Aeronautics and Space Administration, and the National Security Agency.

According to the *Occupational Outlook Handbook*, employment of mathematicians is expected to decline through 2014. The employment outlook in math and physics will not change much within the next few years—particularly for those whose educational background is solely in mathematics. Those who also study related disciplines, such as statistics, computer science, or other types of applied mathematics, will find more opportunities in areas such as computer programming, operations research, and engineering design. Mathematicians may also find employment in industry and government.

According to the American Society of Physics, the outlook for physics employment is not strong. Lately, there has been an oversupply of Ph.D. physicists looking for work and a continued slowdown in civilian physics-related basic research. Competition is also strong for math and physics research jobs in colleges and universities and other centers of research. These trends will result in slower-than-average growth in the employment of physicists and astronomers through 2014. However, defense-related research funded by the government is likely to increase over the next decade, creating some new opportunities for physicists. Additionally, a physics education is good preparation for jobs in information technology, semiconductor technology, and other applied sciences, but job titles are likely to be computer software engineer, computer programmer, engineer, and systems developer, rather than physicist.

Each article in *Careers in Focus: Mathematics and Physics* discusses a particular mathematics- and physics-related occupation in detail. The articles appear in Ferguson's *Encyclopedia of Careers and Vocational Guidance,* but have been updated and revised with the latest information from the U.S. Department of Labor, professional organizations, and other sources. The following paragraphs detail the sections and features that appear in the book.

The **Quick Facts** section provides a brief summary of the career including recommended school subjects, personal skills, work environment, minimum educational requirements, salary ranges, certification or licensing requirements, and employment outlook. This section also provides acronyms and identification numbers for the following government classification indexes: the *Dictionary of Occupational Titles* (DOT), the *Guide for Occupational Exploration* (GOE), the National Occupational Classification (NOC) Index, and the Occupational Information Network (O*NET)-Standard Occupational Classification System (SOC) index. The DOT, GOE, and O*NET-SOC indexes have been created by the U.S. government; the NOC index is Canada's career classification system. Readers can use the identification numbers listed in the Quick Facts section to access further information about a career. Print editions of the DOT

(*Dictionary of Occupational Titles*. Indianapolis, Ind.: JIST Works, 1991) and GOE (*Guide for Occupational Exploration*. Indianapolis, Ind.: JIST Works, 2001) are available at libraries. Electronic versions of the NOC (http://www23.hrdc-drhc.gc.ca) and O*NET-SOC (http://online.onetcenter.org) are available on the Internet. When no DOT, GOE, NOC, or O*NET-SOC numbers are present, this means that the U.S. Department of Labor or Human Resources Development Canada have not created a numerical designation for this career. In this instance, you will see the acronym "N/A," or not available.

The **Overview** section is a brief introductory description of the duties and responsibilities involved in this career. Oftentimes, a career may have a variety of job titles. When this is the case, alternative career titles are presented. The **History** section describes the history of the particular job as it relates to the overall development of its industry or field. **The Job** describes the primary and secondary duties of the job. **Requirements** discusses high school and post-secondary education and training requirements, any certification or licensing that is necessary, and other personal requirements for success in the job. **Exploring** offers suggestions on how to gain experience in or knowledge of the particular job before making a firm educational and financial commitment. The focus is on what can be done while still in high school (or in the early years of college) to gain a better understanding of the job. The **Employers** section gives an overview of typical places of employment for the job. **Starting Out** discusses the best ways to land that first job, be it through the college career services office, newspaper ads, Internet employment sites, or personal contact. The **Advancement** section describes what kind of career path to expect from the job and how to get there. **Earnings** lists salary ranges and describes the typical fringe benefits. The **Work Environment** section describes the typical surroundings and conditions of employment—whether indoors or outdoors, noisy or quiet, social or independent. Also discussed are typical hours worked, any seasonal fluctuations, and the stresses and strains of the job. The **Outlook** section summarizes the job in terms of the general economy and industry projections. For the most part, Outlook information is obtained from the U.S. Bureau of Labor Statistics and is supplemented by information taken from professional associations. Job growth terms follow those used in the *Occupational Outlook Handbook*. Growth described as "much faster than the average" means an increase of 27 percent or more. Growth described as "faster than the average" means an increase of 18 to 26 percent. Growth described as "about as fast as the average" means an increase of 9 to 17 percent. Growth described as "more slowly than the average" means an increase of zero to 8 percent. "Decline" means a decrease by any amount. Each article ends with **For More Information,** which lists organizations that provide information on training, education, internships, scholarships, and job placement.

Careers in Focus: Mathematics and Physics also includes photographs, informative sidebars, and interviews with professionals in the field.

aspects of business. Administrative officers use this information to make sound business decisions.

Budget accountants review expenditures of departments within a firm to make sure expenses allotted are not exceeded. They also aid in drafting budgets and may devise and install budget control systems.

Cost accountants determine unit costs of products or services by analyzing records and depreciation data. They classify and record all operating costs so that management can control expenditures.

Property accountants keep records of equipment, buildings, and other property owned or leased by a company. They prepare mortgage schedules and payments as well as appreciation or depreciation statements, which are used for income tax purposes.

Environmental accountants help utilities, manufacturers, and chemical companies set up preventive systems to ensure environmental compliance and provide assistance in the event that legal issues arise.

Systems accountants design and set up special accounting systems for organizations whose needs cannot be handled by standardized procedures. This may involve installing automated or computerized accounting processes and includes instructing personnel in the new methods.

Forensic accountants and auditors use accounting principles and theories to support or oppose claims being made in litigation.

Tax accountants prepare federal, state, or local tax returns of an individual, business, or corporation according to prescribed rates, laws, and regulations. They also may conduct research on the effects of taxes on firm operations and recommend changes to reduce taxes. This is one of the most intricate fields of accounting, and many accountants therefore specialize in one particular phase such as corporate, individual income, or property tax.

Assurance accountants help improve the quality of information for clients in assurance services areas such as electronic commerce, risk assessment, and elder care. This information may be financial or nonfinancial in nature.

Auditors ensure that financial records are accurate, complete, and in compliance with federal laws. To do so they review items in original entry books, including purchase orders, tax returns, billing statements, and other important documents. Auditors may also prepare financial statements for clients and suggest ways to improve productivity and profits. *Internal auditors* conduct the same kind of examination and evaluation for one particular company. Because they are salaried employees of that company, their financial audits then must be certified by a qualified independent auditor. Internal auditors also review procedures and controls, appraise the efficiency and effectiveness of operations, and make sure their companies comply with corporate policies and government regulations.

Tax auditors review financial records and other information provided by taxpayers to determine the appropriate tax liability. State and federal tax auditors usually work in government offices, but they may perform a field audit in a taxpayer's home or office.

Revenue agents are employed by the federal government to examine selected income tax returns and, when necessary, conduct field audits and investigations to verify the information reported and adjust the tax liability accordingly.

Chief bank examiners enforce good banking practices throughout a state. They schedule bank examinations to ensure that financial institutions comply with state laws and, in certain cases, they take steps to protect a bank's solvency and the interests of its depositors and shareholders.

REQUIREMENTS

High School

If you are interested in an accounting career, you must be very proficient in arithmetic and basic algebra. Familiarity with computers and their applications is equally important. Course work in English and communications will also be beneficial.

Postsecondary Training

Postsecondary training in accounting may be obtained in a wide variety of institutions such as private business schools, junior colleges, universities, and correspondence schools. A bachelor's degree with a major in accounting, or a related field such as economics, is highly recommended by professional associations for those entering the field and is required by all states before taking the licensing exam. It is possible, however, to become a successful accountant by completing a program at any of the above-mentioned institutions. A four-year college curriculum usually includes about two years of liberal arts courses, a year of general business subjects, and a year of specific accounting work. Better positions, particularly in public accounting, require a bachelor's degree with a major in accounting. Large public accounting firms often prefer people with a master's degree in accounting. For beginning positions in accounting, the federal government requires four years of college (including 24 semester hours in accounting or auditing) or an equivalent combination of education and experience.

Certification or Licensing

Certified public accountants (*CPAs*) must pass a qualifying examination and hold a certificate issued by the state in which they wish to practice. In most states, a college degree is required for admission to the CPA examinations; a few states allow candidates to substitute years of public accounting experience for the college degree requirement. Currently 42 states and the District of Columbia require CPA candidates to have 150 hours of education, which is an additional 30 hours beyond the standard bachelor's degree. Five additional states plan to enact the 150-hour requirement in the future. These criteria can be met by combining an undergraduate accounting program with graduate study or participating in an integrated five-year professional accounting program. You can obtain information from a state board of accountancy or check out the Web site of the American Institute of Certified Public Accountants (AICPA) to read about new regulations and review last year's exam.

The Uniform CPA Examination administered by the AICPA is used by all states. Nearly all states require at least two years of public accounting experience or its equivalent before a CPA certificate can be earned.

The AICPA offers additional credentialing programs (involving a test and additional requirements) for members with valid CPA certificates. These designations include accredited in business valuation, certified information technology professional, and personal financial specialist. These credentials indicate that a CPA has developed skills in nontraditional areas in which accountants are starting to play larger roles.

Some accountants seek out other credentials. Those who have earned a bachelor's degree, pass a four-part examination, agree to meet continuing education requirements, and have at least two years of experience in management accounting may become a certified management accountant through the Institute of Management Accounting.

The Accreditation Council for Accountancy and Taxation confers the following designations: accredited business accountant or accredited business advisor, accredited tax preparer, accredited tax advisor, and elder care specialist.

To become a certified internal auditor, college graduates with two years of experience in internal auditing must pass a four-part examination given by the Institute of Internal Auditors (IIA). The IIA also offers the following specialty certifications: certified financial services auditor and certified government auditing professional. Visit the IIA Web site for more information.

The designation certified information systems auditor is conferred by the Information Systems Audit and Control Association to candidates who pass an examination and who have at least five years of experience auditing electronic data processing systems.

Other organizations, such as the Bank Administration Institute, confer specialized auditing designations, including the certified bank auditor designation.

Other Requirements

To be a successful accountant you will need strong mathematical, analytical, and problem-solving skills. You need to be able to think logically and to interpret facts and figures accurately. Effective oral and written communication skills are also essential in working with both clients and management.

Other important skills are attentiveness to detail, patience, and industriousness. Business acumen and the ability to generate clientele are crucial to service-oriented businesses, as are honesty, dedication, and a respect for the work of others.

EXPLORING

If you think a career as an accountant or auditor might be for you, try working in a retail business, either part time or during the summer. Working at the cash register or even pricing products as a stockperson is good introductory experience. You should also consider working as a treasurer for a student organization requiring financial planning and money management. It may be possible to gain some experience by volunteering with local groups such as churches and small businesses. You should also stay abreast of news in the field by reading trade magazines and checking out the industry Web sites of the AICPA and other accounting associations. The AICPA has numerous free educational publications available.

EMPLOYERS

More than 1.1 million people are employed as accountants and auditors. Accountants and auditors work throughout private industry and government. About one quarter work for accounting, auditing, and bookkeeping firms. Approximately 10 percent are self-employed. A large percentage of all accountants and auditors are certified.

STARTING OUT

Junior public accountants usually start in jobs with routine duties such as counting cash, verifying calculations, and other detailed numerical work. In private accounting, beginners are likely to start as cost accountants and junior internal auditors. They may also enter in clerical positions as cost clerks, ledger clerks, and timekeepers or as trainees in technical or junior executive positions. In the federal government, most beginners are hired as trainees at the GS-5 level after passing the civil service exam.

Some state CPA societies arrange internships for accounting majors, and some offer scholarships and loan programs.

You might also visit the Career Development and Workplace Issues section of the AICPA's Web site (http://www.aicpa.org). It has detailed information on accounting careers, hiring trends, job search strategies, resumes and cover letters, and job interviews. The Becoming a CPA/Academic Resources section also has a list of internship and scholarship opportunities for students as well as a Landing a Job link.

ADVANCEMENT

Talented accountants and auditors can advance quickly. Junior public accountants usually advance to senior positions within several years and to managerial positions soon after. Those successful in dealing with top-level management may eventually become supervisors, managers, and partners in larger firms or go into independent practice. However, only 2 to 3 percent of new hires advance to audit manager, tax manager, or partner.

Private accountants in firms may become audit managers, tax managers, cost accounting managers, or controllers, depending on their specialty. Some become controllers, treasurers, or corporation presidents. Others on the finance side may rise to become managers of financial planning and analysis or treasurers.

Federal government trainees are usually promoted within a year or two. Advancement to controller and to higher administrative positions is ultimately possible.

Although advancement may be rapid for skilled accountants, especially in public accounting, those with inadequate academic or professional training are often assigned to routine jobs and find it difficult to obtain promotions. All accountants find it necessary to continue their study of accounting and related areas in their spare time. Even those who have already obtained college degrees, gained experience, and earned a CPA certificate may spend many hours studying to keep up with new industry developments. Thousands of practicing accountants enroll in formal courses offered by universities and professional associations to specialize in certain areas of accounting, broaden or update their professional skills, and become eligible for advancement and promotion.

EARNINGS

Average beginning salaries for accountants with a bachelor's degree were $43,269 a year in 2005; those with a master's degree averaged $46,251 a year, according to the National Association of Colleges and Employers. Auditors with up to one year of experience earned between $28,250 and $45,000, according to a 2005 survey by Robert Half International. Some experienced auditors may earn between $52,000 and $200,000, depending on such factors as their education level, the size of the firm, and the firm's location.

According to the U.S. Department of Labor, accountants and auditors had median annual earnings of $54,630 in 2006. The lowest paid 10 percent earned less than $34,470, and the highest paid 10 percent earned more than $94,050. In the federal government, the average starting salary for junior accountants and auditors was $24,677 in 2005. Entry-level candidates who had a superior academic record received offers of $30,567. Accountants working for the federal government had mean salaries of $62,170 a year in 2005; auditors averaged $78,890. Although government accountants and auditors make less than those in other areas, they do receive more benefits.

Accountants in large firms and with large corporations receive typical benefits including paid vacation and sick days, insurance, and savings and pension plans. Employees in smaller companies generally receive fewer fringe benefits.

WORK ENVIRONMENT

Accounting is known as a desk job, and a 40-hour (or longer) workweek can be expected in public and private accounting. Although computer work is replacing paperwork, the job can be routine and monotonous, and concentration and attention to detail are critical. Public accountants experience considerable pressure during the tax period, which runs from November to April, and they may have to work long hours. There is potential for stress aside from tax season, as accountants can be responsible for managing multimillion-dollar finances with no margin for error. Self-employed accountants and those working for a small firm can expect to work longer hours; 40 percent work more than 50 hours per week, compared to 20 percent of public and private accountants.

In smaller firms, most of the public accountant's work is performed in the client's office. A considerable amount of travel is often necessary to service a wide variety of businesses. In a larger firm, however, an accountant may have very little client contact, spending more time interacting with the accounting team.

OUTLOOK

Employment of accountants and auditors is expected to grow faster than the average for all occupations through 2014, according to the U.S. Department of Labor. This is due to business growth, changing tax and finance laws, and increased scrutiny of financial practices across all businesses. There have been several notable scandals in the accounting industry in recent years, and this accounts for much of the increased scrutiny and changing legislation in this industry.

As firms specialize their services, accountants will need to follow suit. Firms will seek out accountants with experience in marketing and proficiency in computer systems to build management consulting practices. As trade increases, so will the demand for CPAs with international specialties and foreign language skills. CPAs with an engineering degree would be well equipped to specialize in environmental accounting. Other accounting specialties that will enjoy good prospects include assurance, forensic, and tax accounting.

The number of CPAs dropped off a bit after most states embraced the 150-hour standard for CPA education. However, numbers are once again starting to rise as students realize the many opportunities this industry holds, especially in the wake of recent accounting scandals. CPAs with valid licenses should experience favorable job prospects for the foreseeable future. Pursuing advanced degrees and certifications will also greatly increase one's chances of finding employment.

Accounting jobs are more secure than most during economic downswings. Despite fluctuations in the nation's economy, there will always be a need to manage financial information, especially as the number, size, and complexity of business transactions increases. However, competition for jobs will remain, certification requirements will become more rigorous, and accountants and auditors with the highest degrees will be the most competitive.

FOR MORE INFORMATION

For information on accreditation and testing, contact
Accreditation Council for Accountancy and Taxation
1010 North Fairfax Street
Alexandria, VA 22314-1574
Tel: 888-289-7763

Email: info@acatcredentials.org
http://www.acatcredentials.org

*For information on the Uniform CPA Examination and student
membership, contact*
American Institute of Certified Public Accountants
1211 Avenue of the Americas
New York, NY 10036-8775
Tel: 212-596-6200
http://www.aicpa.org

For information on accredited programs in accounting, contact
Association to Advance Collegiate Schools of Business
777 South Harbour Island Boulevard, Suite 750
Tampa, FL 33602-5730
Tel: 813-769-6500
http://www.aacsb.edu

For information on certification for bank auditors, contact
Bank Administration Institute
One North Franklin, Suite 1000
Chicago, IL 60606-3421
Tel: 888-284-4078
Email: info@bai.org
http://www.bai.org

For more information on women in accounting, contact
The Educational Foundation for Women in Accounting
PO Box 1925
Southeastern, PA 19399-1925
Tel: 610-407-9229
Email: info@efwa.org
http://www.efwa.org

For information on certification, contact
Information Systems Audit and Control Association and
    Foundation
3701 Algonquin Road, Suite 1010
Rolling Meadows, IL 60008-3124
Tel: 847-253-1545
Email: certification@isaca.org
http://www.isaca.org

For information on internal auditing and certification, contact
The Institute of Internal Auditors
247 Maitland Avenue
Altamonte Springs, FL 32701-4201
Tel: 407-937-1100
Email: iia@theiia.org
http://www.theiia.org

For information about management accounting and the certified management accountant designation, as well as student membership, contact
Institute of Management Accountants
10 Paragon Drive
Montvale, NJ 07645-1718
Tel: 800-638-4427
Email: ima@imanet.org
http://www.imanet.org

Actuaries

QUICK FACTS

School Subjects
Business
Mathematics

Personal Skills
Following instructions
Leadership/management

Work Environment
Primarily indoors
One location with some
travel

Minimum Education Level
Bachelor's degree

Salary Range
$46,470 to $82,800 to
$145,600+

Certification or Licensing
Required

Outlook
Faster than the average

DOT
020

GOE
02.06.02

NOC
2161

O*NET-SOC
15-2011.00

OVERVIEW

Actuaries use statistical formulas and techniques to calculate the probability of events such as death, disability, sickness, unemployment, retirement, and property loss. Actuaries develop formulas to predict how much money an insurance company will pay in claims, which determines the overall cost of insuring a group, business, or individual. Increase in risk raises potential cost to the company, which, in turn, raises its rates. Actuaries analyze risk to estimate the number and amount of claims an insurance company will have to pay. They assess the cost of running the business and incorporate the results into the design and evaluation of programs.

Casualty actuaries specialize in property and liability insurance; *life actuaries* in health and life insurance. In recent years, there has been an increase in the number of actuaries—called *pension actuaries*—who deal only with pension plans. The total number of actuaries employed in the United States is approximately 18,000.

HISTORY

The term actuary was used for the first time in 1762 in the charter for the Equitable Society of London, which was the first life insurance company to use scientific data in figuring premiums. The basis of actuarial work was laid in the early 17th century when Frenchmen Blaise Pascal and Pierre de Fermat derived an important method of calculating actuarial probabilities, resulting in what is now termed the science of probability.

The first mortality table was produced in the late 17th century, when Edmund Halley noticed the regularity of various social phenomena, including the excess of male over female births. Halley, an English astronomer for whom Halley's comet is named, is known as the father of life insurance. As more complex forms of insurance were developed in the 19th century, the need for actuaries grew.

In 1889, a small group of qualified actuaries formed the Actuarial Society of America. Two classes of members, fellows and associates, were created seven years later, and special examinations were developed to determine membership eligibility. Forms of these examinations are still used today. By 1909 the American Institute of Actuaries was created, and in 1949 these two groups consolidated into the present Society of Actuaries.

In 1911, the Casualty Actuary Society was formed in response to the development of workers' compensation laws. The compensation laws opened up many new fields of insurance, and the Casualty Actuarial Society has since moved into all aspects of property and liability insurance.

OASDI (Old Age, Survivors, and Disability Insurance), now known as Social Security, was created in 1935 and expanded the work of pension actuaries. The creation of this program greatly impacted the development, philosophy, and structure of private pension programs. The American Society of Pension Actuaries (now known as the American Society of Pension Professionals and Actuaries) was formed in 1966; its members provide services to over 30 percent of the qualified retirement plans in the United States.

The first actuaries were concerned primarily with statistical, mathematical, and financial calculations needed in the rapidly growing field. Today they deal with problems of investment, selection of risk factors for insurance, agents' compensation, social insurance, taxation, development of policy forms, and many other aspects of insurance. Once considered mathematicians, actuaries are now referred to as "financial architects" and "social mathematicians" because they use their unique combination of numerical, analytical, and business skills to solve a variety of social and financial problems.

THE JOB

Should smokers pay more for their health insurance? Should younger drivers pay higher car insurance premiums? Actuaries answer questions like these to ensure that insurance and pension organizations can pay their claims and maintain a profitable business.

Using their knowledge of mathematics, probability, statistics, and principles of finance and business, actuaries determine premium rates and the various benefits of insurance plans. To accomplish this task, they first assemble and analyze statistics on birth, death, marriage, parenthood, employment, and other pertinent facts and figures. Based on this information, they are able to develop mathematical models of rates of death, accident, sickness, disability, or retirement and then construct tables regarding the probability of such things as property loss from fire, theft, accident, or natural disaster. After calculating all probabilities and the resulting costs to the company, the actuaries can determine the premium rates to allow insurance companies to cover predicted losses, turn a profit, and remain competitive with other businesses.

For example, based on analyses, actuaries are able to determine how many of each 1,000 people 21 years of age are expected to survive to age 65. They can calculate how many of them are expected to die this year or how many are expected to live until age 85. The probability that an insured person may die during the period before reaching 65 is a risk to the company. The actuaries must figure a price for the premium that will cover all claims and expenses as they occur and still earn a profit for the company assuming the risk. In the same way, actuaries calculate premium rates and determine policy provisions for every type of insurance coverage.

Employment opportunities span across the variety of different types of insurance companies, including life, health, accident, automobile, fire, or workers' compensation organizations. Most actuaries specialize either as casualty actuaries, dealing with property and liability insurance, or as life actuaries, working with life and health

Earnings by Specialty, 2006

Industry	Mean Annual Earnings
Management and technical consulting services	$102,750
Accounting, tax preparation, bookkeeping, and payroll services	$99,150
Insurance agencies, brokerages, and related companies	$97,570
Federal government	$96,220
Insurance carriers	$89,040
Management of companies and enterprises	$86,750
State government	$73,780

Source: U.S. Department of Labor

insurance. In addition, actuaries may concentrate on pension plan programs sponsored and administered by various levels of government, private business, or fraternal or benevolent associations.

Actuaries work in many departments in insurance companies, including underwriting, group insurance, investment, pension, sales, and service. In addition to their own company's business, they analyze characteristics of the insurance business as a whole. They study general economic and social trends as well as legislative, health, and other developments, all of which may affect insurance practices. With this broad knowledge, some actuaries reach executive positions, where they can influence and help determine company policy and develop new lines of business. *Actuary executives* may communicate with government officials, company executives, policyholders, or the public to explain complex technical matters. They may testify before public agencies regarding proposed legislation that has a bearing on the insurance business, for example, or they may explain proposed changes in premium rates or contract provisions.

Actuaries may also work with a consulting firm, providing advice to clients including insurance companies, corporations, hospitals, labor unions, and government agencies. They develop employee benefits, calculating future benefits and employer contributions, and set up pension and welfare plans. *Consulting actuaries* also advise health care and financial services firms, and they may work with small insurance companies lacking an actuarial department.

Since the government regulates the insurance industry and administers laws on pensions, it also requires the services of actuaries to determine whether companies are complying with the law. A small number of actuaries are employed by the federal government and deal with Social Security, Medicare, disability and life insurance, and pension plans for veterans, members of the armed forces, and federal employees. Those in state governments may supervise and regulate insurance companies, oversee the operations of state retirement or pension systems, and manage problems related to unemployment insurance and workers' compensation.

REQUIREMENTS
High School
If you are interested in this field, you should pursue a traditional college preparatory curriculum including mathematical and computer science classes and also take advantage of advanced courses such as calculus. Introductory business, economics, accounting, and finance courses are important, as is English to develop your oral and written skills.

Postsecondary Training

A bachelor's degree with a major in actuarial science, mathematics, or statistics is highly recommended for entry into the industry. Courses in elementary and advanced algebra, differential and integral calculus, descriptive and analytical statistics, principles of mathematical statistics, probability, and numerical analysis are all important. Computer science is also a vital part of actuarial training. Employers are increasingly hiring graduates with majors in economics, business, and engineering who have a strong math background. College students should broaden their education to include business, economics, and finance as well as English and communications. Because actuarial work revolves around social and political issues, course work in the humanities and social sciences will also prove useful.

Certification or Licensing

Full professional status in an actuarial specialty is based on completing a series of 10 examinations. Success is based on both formal and on-the-job training. Actuaries can become associate members of the Society of Actuaries after successfully completing seven of the 10 examinations for the life and health insurance, finance, and pension fields. Similarly, they can reach associate status in the Casualty Actuarial Society after successfully completing seven out of 10 exams in the property and liability field. Most actuaries achieve associateship in three to five years. Actuaries who successfully complete the entire series of exams for either organization are granted full membership and become fellows.

The American Society of Pension Professionals and Actuaries also offers several different designations (both actuarial and non-actuarial) to individuals who pass the required examinations in the pension field and have the appropriate work experience.

Consulting pension actuaries who service private pension plans must be enrolled and licensed by the Joint Board for the Enrollment of Actuaries (http://www.irs.gov/taxpros/actuaries), a U.S. government agency. Only these actuaries can work with pension plans set up under the Employee Retirement Income Security Act. To be accepted, applicants must meet certain professional and educational requirements stipulated by the Joint Board.

Completion of the entire series of exams may take from five to 10 years. Because the first exams offered by these various boards and societies cover core material (such as calculus, linear algebra, probability and statistics, risk theory, and actuarial math), students generally wait to commit to a specialty until they have taken the initial tests. Students pursuing a career as an actuary should complete the first two or three preliminary examinations while still in college, since these tests cover subjects usually taught in school; the more advanced examinations cover aspects of the profession itself.

Employers prefer to hire individuals who have already passed the first two exams. Once employed, companies generally give employees time during the workday to study. They may also pay exam fees, provide study materials, and award raises upon an employee's successful completion of an exam.

Other Requirements

An aptitude in mathematics, statistics, and computer science is a must to become a successful actuary, as are sound analytical and problem-solving skills. Solid oral and written communication skills are also required in order to be able to explain and interpret complex work to the client, as is skill with programming languages such as Visual Basic.

Prospective actuaries should also have an inquisitive mind with an interest in historical, social, and political issues and trends. You should have a general feel for the business world and be able to assimilate a wide range of complex information in order to see the "big picture" when planning policies. Actuaries like to solve problems; they are strategists who enjoy and generally excel at games such as chess. Actuaries need to be motivated and self-disciplined to concentrate on detailed work, especially under stress, and to undertake the rigorous study for licensing examinations.

EXPLORING

If you think you are interested in the actuarial field, try pursuing extracurricular opportunities that allow you to practice strategic thinking and problem-solving skills; these may include chess, math, or investment clubs at your school. Other activities that foster leadership and management, such as student council positions, will also be beneficial. Any kind of business or research-oriented summer or part-time experience will be valuable, especially with an accounting or law firm.

There are more than 45 local actuarial clubs and regional affiliates throughout the United States that offer opportunities for informal discussion and networking. Talk with people in the field to better understand the nature of the work, and use the association's resources to learn more about the field. The Society of Actuaries offers free educational publications.

College undergraduates can take advantage of summer internships and employment in insurance companies and consulting firms.

Students will have the chance to rotate among jobs to learn various actuarial operations and different phases of insurance work.

EMPLOYERS

There are approximately 18,000 actuaries employed in the United States, and about six out of 10 work in the insurance industry. Other actuaries work for financial service-providing firms including commercial banks, investment banks, and retirement funds. Others are employed by actuarial consulting services and in academia. Some actuaries are self-employed.

STARTING OUT

The best way to enter this field is by taking the necessary beginning examinations while still in college. Once students have graduated and passed these exams, they are in a very good position to apply for entry-level jobs in the field and can command higher starting salaries. Some college students organize interviews and find jobs through their college career services office, while others interview with firms recruiting on campus. Many firms offer summer and year-round actuarial training programs or internships that may result in a full-time job.

Beginning actuaries may prepare calculations for actuarial tables or work with policy settlements or funds. With experience, they may prepare correspondence, reports, and research. Beginners who have already passed the preliminary exams often start with more responsibility and higher pay.

ADVANCEMENT

Advancement within the profession to assistant, associate, or chief actuary greatly depends on the individual's on-the-job performance, competence on the actuarial examinations, and leadership capabilities.

Some actuaries qualify for administrative positions in underwriting, accounting, or investment because of their broad business knowledge and specific insurance experience. Because their judgment is so valuable, actuaries may advance to administrative or executive positions, such as head of a department, vice president or president of a company, manager of an insurance rating bureau, partner in a consulting firm, or, possibly, state insurance commissioner. Actuaries with management skills and a strong business background may move into other areas such as marketing, advertising, and planning.

EARNINGS

Starting salaries for actuaries with bachelor's degrees in actuarial science averaged $52,741 in 2005, according to a survey conducted by the National Association of Colleges and Employers. New college graduates who have not passed any actuarial examinations earn slightly less. Insurance companies and consulting firms offer merit increases or bonuses to those who pass examinations.

The U.S. Department of Labor reports that actuaries earned a median annual salary of $82,800 in 2006. Ten percent earned less than $46,470, while the top 25 percent earned more than $145,600. Actuaries working for insurance companies receive paid vacations, health and life insurance, pension plans, and other fringe benefits.

WORK ENVIRONMENT

Actuaries spend much of their 40-hour workweek behind a desk poring over facts and figures, although some travel to various units of the organization or to other businesses. This is especially true of the consulting actuary, who will most likely work longer hours and travel more. Consulting actuaries tend to have more diverse work and more personal interaction in working with a variety of clients. Though the work can be stressful and demands intense concentration and attention to detail, actuaries find their jobs to be rewarding and satisfying and feel that they make a direct and positive impact on people's lives.

OUTLOOK

The U.S. Department of Labor predicts faster than average growth for the actuary field through 2014. Growth of the insurance industry—traditionally the leading employer of actuaries—is expected to remain steady, with many new fields such as annuities and terrorism-related property-risk analysis, compensating for the shrinking life insurance industry. The field's stringent entrance requirements and competition for entry-level jobs will also continue to restrict the number of candidates for jobs.

The insurance industry continues to evolve, and actuaries will be in demand to establish rates in several new areas of coverage, including prepaid legal, dental, and kidnapping insurance. In many cases, actuarial data that have been supplied by rating bureaus are now being developed in new actuarial departments created in companies affected by states' new competitive rating laws. Other new areas of insurance coverage that will involve actuaries include product and pollution liability insurance as well as greater workers' compensation and medical malpractice coverage. Insurers will call on actuaries to help them respond to new state and federal regulations while cutting costs, especially in the areas of pension reform and no-fault automobile insurance. In the future, actuaries will also be employed by non-insurance businesses or will work in business- and investment-related fields. Some are already working in banking and finance.

Actuaries will be needed to assess the financial impact of current issues such as AIDS, terrorism, and the changing health care system. As demographics change, people live and work longer, and as medicine advances, actuaries will need to reexamine the probabilities of death, sickness, and retirement.

Casualty actuaries will find more work as companies find themselves held responsible for product liability. In the wake of recent environmental disasters, there will also be a growing need to evaluate environmental risk.

As business goes global, it presents a whole new set of risks and problems as economies develop and new markets emerge. As private enterprise expands in the former Soviet Union, how does a company determine the risk of opening, say, a department store in Moscow?

Actuaries are no longer just mathematical experts. With their unique combination of analytical and business skills, their role is expanding as they become broad-based business professionals solving social as well as financial problems.

FOR MORE INFORMATION

For general information about actuary careers, contact
American Academy of Actuaries
1100 17th Street, NW, 7th Floor
Washington, DC 20036-4601
Tel: 202-223-8196
http://www.actuary.org

For information about continuing education and professional designations, contact
American Society of Pension Professionals and Actuaries
4245 North Fairfax Drive, Suite 750
Arlington, VA 22203-1648
Tel: 703-516-9300
Email: asppa@asppa.org
http://www.asppa.org

The Be An Actuary section of the CAS Web site offers comprehensive information on the career of actuary.
Casualty Actuarial Society (CAS)
4350 North Fairfax Drive, Suite 250
Arlington, VA 22203-1695
Tel: 703-276-3100
Email: office@casact.org
http://www.casact.org

For information about continuing education and professional designations, contact
Society of Actuaries
475 North Martingale Road, Suite 600
Schaumburg, IL 60173-2252
Tel: 847-706-3500
http://www.soa.org

Architects

QUICK FACTS

School Subjects
Art
Mathematics

Personal Skills
Artistic
Communication/ideas

Work Environment
Primarily indoors
Primarily one location

Minimum Education Level
Bachelor's degree

Salary Range
$39,420 to $64,150 to
$104,970+

Certification or Licensing
Voluntary (certification)
Required (licensing)

Outlook
About as fast as the average

DOT
001

GOE
02.07.03

NOC
2151

O*NET-SOC
17-1011.00

OVERVIEW

Architects plan, design, and observe construction of facilities used for human occupancy and of other structures. They consult with clients, plan layouts of buildings, prepare drawings of proposed buildings, write specifications, and prepare scale and full-sized drawings. Architects also may help clients to obtain bids, select a contractor, and negotiate the construction contract, and they also visit construction sites to ensure that the work is being completed according to specification. There are approximately 129,000 architects working in the United States.

HISTORY

Architecture began not with shelters for people to live in but with the building of religious structures—from Stonehenge in England and the pyramids in Egypt to pagodas in Japan and the Parthenon in Greece. It was the Romans who developed a new building method—concrete vaulting—that made possible large cities with permanent masonry buildings. As they extended the Roman Empire, they built for public and military purposes. They developed and built apartment buildings, law courts, public baths, theaters, and circuses. The industrial revolution with its demand for factories and mills developed iron and steel construction, which evolved into the steel and glass skyscraper of today.

Because the history of architecture follows that of human civilization, the architecture of any period reflects the culture of its people. Architecture of early periods has influenced that of later centuries, including the work of contemporary architects. The field continues to develop as new techniques and materials are discovered and as architects blend creativity with function.

THE JOB

The architect normally has two responsibilities: to design a building that will satisfy the client and to protect the public's health, safety, and welfare. This second responsibility requires architects to be licensed by the state in which they work. Meeting the first responsibility involves many steps. The job begins with learning what the client wants. The architect takes many factors into consideration, including local and state building and design regulations, climate, soil on which the building is to be constructed, zoning laws, fire regulations, and the client's financial limitations.

The architect then prepares a set of plans that, upon the client's approval, will be developed into final design and construction documents. The final design shows the exact dimensions of every portion of the building, including the location and size of columns and beams, electrical outlets and fixtures, plumbing, heating and air-conditioning facilities, windows, and doors. The architect works closely with consulting engineers on the specifics of the plumbing, heating, air-conditioning, and electrical work to be done.

The architect then assists the client in getting bids from general contractors, one of whom will be selected to construct the building to the specifications. The architect helps the client through the completion of the construction and occupancy phases, making certain the correct materials are used and that the drawings and specifications are faithfully followed.

Throughout the process the architect works closely with a design or project team. This team is usually made up of the following: *designers,* who specialize in design development; a *structural designer,* who designs the frame of the building in accordance with the work of the architect; the *project manager* or *job superintendent,* who sees that the full detail drawings are completed to the satisfaction of the architect; and the *specification writer* and *estimator,* who prepare a project manual that describes in more detail the materials to be used in the building, their quality and method of installation, and all details related to the construction of the building.

The architect's job is very complex. He or she is expected to know construction methods, engineering principles and practices, and materials. Architects also must be up to date on new design and construction techniques and procedures. Although architects once spent most of their time designing buildings for the wealthy, they are now more often involved in the design of housing developments, individual dwellings, supermarkets, industrial plants, office buildings, shopping centers, air terminals, schools, banks, museums, churches and religious structures of other faiths, and dozens of other types of buildings.

Architects discuss blueprints and a building model with clients. *(David R. Frazier, The Image Works)*

Architects may specialize in any one of a number of fields, including building appraisal, city planning, teaching, architectural journalism, furniture design, lighting design, or government service. Regardless of the area of specialization, the architect's major task is that of understanding the client's needs and then reconciling them into a meaningful whole.

REQUIREMENTS

High School

To prepare for this career while in high school, take a college preparatory program that includes courses in English, mathematics, physics, art (especially freehand drawing), social studies, history, and foreign languages. Courses in business and computer science also will be useful.

Postsecondary Training

Because most state architecture registration boards require a professional degree, high school students are advised, early in their senior year, to apply for admission to a professional program that is accredited by the National Architectural Accrediting Board. Competition to enter these programs is high. Grades, class rank, and aptitude and achievement scores count heavily in determining who will be accepted.

Most schools of architecture offer degrees through either a five-year bachelor's program or a three- or four-year master's program. The majority of architecture students seek out the bachelor's degree in architecture, going from high school directly into a five-year program. Though this is the fastest route, you should be certain that you want to study architecture. Because the programs are so specialized, it is difficult to transfer to another field of study if you change your mind. The master's degree option allows for more flexibility but takes longer to complete. In this case, students first earn a liberal arts degree and then continue their training by completing a master's program in architecture.

A typical college architecture program includes courses in architectural history and theory, the technical and legal aspects of building design, science, and liberal arts.

Certification or Licensing

All states and the District of Columbia require that individuals be licensed before contracting to provide architectural services in that particular state.

Licensure requirements include graduation from an accredited school of architecture, three years of practical experience (called an internship) with a licensed architect, and passing the rigorous Architect Registration Examination. Some states require architects to maintain their licensing through continued education. These individuals may complete a certain number of credits every year or two through seminars, workshops, university classes, self-study courses, or other sources.

In addition to becoming licensed, a growing number of architects choose to obtain certification by the National Council of Architectural Registration Boards. If an architect plans to work in more than one state, obtaining this certification can make it easier to become licensed in different states.

Other Requirements

If you are interested in architecture, you should be intelligent, observant, responsible, and self-disciplined. You should have a concern for detail and accuracy, be able to communicate effectively both orally and in writing, and be able to accept criticism constructively. Although great artistic ability is not necessary, you should be able to visualize spatial relationships and have the capacity to solve technical problems. Mathematical ability is also important. In addition, you should possess organizational skills and leadership qualities and be able to work well with others.

EXPLORING

Most architects will welcome the opportunity to talk with young people interested in entering architecture. You may be able to visit

Additional Career Options for Architects

An architecture education can lead to a variety of interesting careers beyond that of a traditional career at an architecture firm. Consider the following options as you contemplate a career in architecture:

- architecture critic
- architectural photographer
- architecture professor
- architectural programmer
- architectural renderer
- building inspector
- building pathologist
- campus planner
- carpenter
- cartographer
- city planner
- civil engineer
- computer-aided-design coordinator
- construction inspector
- construction manager
- contractor
- corporate consultant

- design/build team manager
- environmental planner
- furniture designer
- graphic designer
- historic preservationist
- illustrator
- industrial designer
- landscape architect
- lawyer
- museum curator
- property assessor
- real estate agent
- real estate developer
- researcher
- set designer
- structural engineer
- technical writer

Source: American Institute of Architecture Students

their offices to gain a firsthand knowledge of the type of work done by architects. You can also visit a design studio of a school of architecture or work for an architect or building contractor during summer vacations. Also, many architecture schools offer summer programs for high school students. Books and magazines on architecture also can give you a broad understanding of the nature of the work and the values of the profession.

EMPLOYERS

Of the 129,000 architects working in the United States, most are employed by architectural firms or other firms related to the construction industry. About one in four architects, however, are self-employed—the ultimate dream of many people in the profession. A few develop graphic design, interior design, or product specialties. Still others put their training to work in the theater, film, or television fields, or in museums, display firms, and architectural product and materials manufacturing companies. A small number are employed in government agencies such as the Departments of Defense, Interior, and Housing and Urban Development and the General Services Administration.

STARTING OUT

Students entering architecture following graduation start as interns in an architectural office. As interns, they assist in preparing architectural construction documents. They also handle related details, such as administering contracts, coordinating the work of other professionals on the project, researching building codes and construction materials, and writing specifications. As an alternative to working for an architectural firm, some architecture graduates go into allied fields such as construction, engineering, interior design, landscape architecture, or real estate development.

ADVANCEMENT

Interns and architects alike are given progressively more complex jobs. Architects may advance to supervisory or managerial positions. Some architects become partners in established firms, while others take steps to establish their own practice.

EARNINGS

Architects earned a median annual salary of $64,150 in 2006, according to the U.S. Department of Labor. The lowest paid 10 percent earned less than $39,420 annually, while the highest paid 10 percent earned $104,970 or more.

Well-established architects who are partners in an architectural firm or who have their own businesses generally earn much more than salaried employees. Most employers offer such fringe benefits as health insurance, sick and vacation pay, and retirement plans.

WORK ENVIRONMENT

Architects normally work a 40-hour week. There may be a number of times when they will have to work overtime, especially when under pressure to complete an assignment. Self-employed architects work less regular hours and often meet with clients in their homes or offices during the evening. Architects usually work in comfortable offices, but they may spend a considerable amount of time outside the office visiting clients or viewing the progress of a particular job in the field. Their routines usually vary considerably.

OUTLOOK

Employment in the field is expected to grow about as fast as the average for all occupations through 2014, according to the U.S. Department of Labor. The number of architects needed will depend on the volume of construction. The construction industry is extremely sensitive to fluctuations in the overall economy, and a bad economic climate could result in layoffs. On the positive side, employment of architects is not likely to be affected by the growing use of computer technologies. Rather than replacing architects, computers are being used to enhance the architect's work.

Competition for employment will continue to be strong, particularly in prestigious architectural firms. Openings will not be newly created positions but will become available as the workload increases and established architects transfer to other occupations or leave the field.

FOR MORE INFORMATION

For information on education, scholarships, and student membership opportunities, contact
American Institute of Architects
1735 New York Avenue, NW
Washington, DC 20006-5292
Tel: 800-242-3837
Email: infocentral@aia.org
http://www.aia.org

For information on education and student membership opportunities, contact
American Institute of Architecture Students
1735 New York Avenue, NW
Washington, DC 20006-5292
Tel: 202-626-7472
Email: mailbox@aias.org
http://www.aias.org

For information on schools of architecture, contact
Association of Collegiate Schools of Architecture
1735 New York Avenue, NW

Washington, DC 20006-5292
Tel: 202-785-2324
http://www.acsa-arch.org

For information on careers in architecture, visit
ARCHcareers.org
http://www.archcareers.org

INTERVIEW

Katherine Austin has been an architect for nearly 20 years. For the past 12 years, she has owned her own firm in Sebastopol, California, that specializes in affordable housing and green building design. Katherine discussed her career with the editors of Careers in Focus: Mathematics and Physics.

Q. Why did you decide to become an architect?

A. For me it was a second career. I switched when I was 30. I had always wanted to be an architect since the seventh grade but was afraid of the math. I did poorly in algebra as a kid, and so I went into fine arts instead. I got a master's degree in fine arts and taught for five years before making the switch. The final thing that made the decision clear was that I found out about a three-year master's program at the University of California-Los Angeles (UCLA). Since I already had a master's, I didn't want to do a five-year undergraduate degree. UCLA was the only place I could afford, too, as I was very poor and underemployed in art.

Q. What do you like most and least about your job?

A. I love what I do. Every day is different, and I can express my creativity. But I work for myself. I established my own firm after working for others for nine years. What I least liked during that time was basically being a slave and working 72 hours a week for a firm that paid me very little for my skills. Unfortunately this is how the profession is set up to treat interns for the first three years. You just need to gut it out and figure that later it will be better. The camaraderie during that time is usually great, and there are things to love even during the tough times.

Q. What are the most important professional qualities for architects?

A. There are many areas that one can focus on within the profession. But to be successful in general you need to be:

- Well educated in aesthetics (i.e., study fine arts, art history, architecture history, and world cultures).
- A really good "people person"—that is, get along well with teams of people, clients, consultants, and include with that excellent communications skills.
- Extremely well organized. You need to be able to keep track of your time and be able to do many things at once or in the course of each day. If you can only focus on one thing at a time, you will not rise to the top.

Q. What advice would you give to high school students who are interested in becoming architects?

A. • Do well in math but don't worry about it too much. In truth, all architects use engineers to do their structural engineering. You only need to know enough to work with the engineer.

- What you need to focus on is learning art (classes in art history and drawing as well as learning as much as possible about other cultures and their buildings).
- Visit as many art museums and cultural history museums as you can.
- Visit beautiful cities and really look at the buildings. Try to figure out what makes them beautiful. Suggested places in the United States are Boston; parts of New York City; Washington, D.C.; Savannah, Georgia; Chicago; Taos, New Mexico; Portland, Oregon; and San Francisco. In Los Angeles, there are many new interesting individual buildings, but the city is not pretty.
- Work on your presentation skills. I recommend taking speech classes—especially if you are shy—or drama.
- Take physics so you have an overall understanding of structural engineering and mechanical systems.
- If you can, participate in a Habitat for Humanity build. That would be great and a big help, too.
- If you can, get a summer job doing work on a construction site. That is great experience. (Don't bother trying to work for an architect; they won't have the time to teach you anything, and they have enough trouble teaching their interns.) Ask to interview a number of different architects in your area and ask them the same questions. Everyone is different, and you will learn a lot.

Assessors and Appraisers

OVERVIEW

Assessors and appraisers collect and interpret data to make judgments about the value, quality, and use of property. Assessors are government officials who evaluate property for the express purpose of determining how much the real estate owner should pay the city or county government in property taxes. Appraisers evaluate the market value of property to help people make decisions about purchases, sales, investments, mortgages, or loans. Rural districts or small towns may have only a few assessors, while large cities or urban counties may have several hundred. Appraisers are especially in demand in large cities but also work in smaller communities. There are approximately 102,000 real estate assessors and appraisers employed in the United States.

HISTORY

Until the 1930s, most assessors and appraisers were lay people using unscientific, informal methods to estimate the value of property. People who were not trained specifically in the field performed appraisals as a part-time adjunct to a general real estate business. As a result, the "boom" period of the 1920s saw many abuses of appraisals, such as approving loans in excess of the property's real value based on inaccurate estimates. The events of the Great Depression in the 1930s further highlighted the need for professionalism in appraising. Real estate owners defaulted on their mortgages, real estate bond issues stopped paying interest, and real estate corporations went into receivership.

In 1922 the National Association of Real Estate Boards (NAREB) defined specializations of its real estate functions to encourage professionalism in the industry. They did not organize an independent appraisal division, however, because there were few appraisers and the industry at large did not appreciate the importance of sound appraisals.

The NAREB recognized appraising as a significant branch of specialization in 1928 but did not formulate clearly defined appraisal standards and appraisal treatises until the 1930s.

Since then, appraising has emerged as a complex profession offering many responsibilities and opportunities. With the advent of computers, assessing and appraising have become more scientific. Today, assessments are based on a combination of economic and statistical analysis and common sense.

People need reliable appraisals when selling, mortgaging, taxing, insuring, or developing real estate. Buyers and sellers of property want to know the property's market value as a guide in their negotiations and may need economic feasibility studies or advice about other investment considerations for a proposed or existing development. Mortgage lenders require appraisals before issuing loans, and insurance companies often need an estimate of value before underwriting a property.

THE JOB

Property is divided into two distinct types: real property and personal property. Real property is land and the structures built upon the land, while personal property includes all other types of possessions. Appraisers determine the value, quality, and use of real property and personal property based on selective research into market areas, the application of analytical techniques, and professional judgment derived from experience. In evaluating real property, they analyze the supply and demand for different types of property, such as residential dwellings, office buildings, shopping centers, industrial sites, and farms, to estimate their values. Appraisers analyze construction, condition, and functional design. They review public records of sales, leases, previous assessments, and other transactions pertaining to land and buildings to determine the market values, rents, and construction costs of similar properties. Appraisers collect information about neighborhoods, such as availability of gas, electricity, power lines, and transportation. They also may interview people familiar with the property, and they consider the cost of making improvements on the property.

Appraisers also must consider such factors as location and changes that might influence the future value of the property. A residence worth $300,000 in the suburbs may be worth only a fraction of that in the inner city or in a remote rural area. But that same suburban residence may depreciate in value if an airport will be built nearby. After conducting a thorough investigation, appraisers usually prepare a written report that documents their findings and conclusions.

Most appraisers deal with land and buildings, but some evaluate other items of value. Specialized appraisers evaluate antiques, gems and jewelry, machinery, equipment, aircraft, boats, oil and gas reserves, and businesses. These appraisers obtain special training in their areas of expertise but generally perform the same functions as real property appraisers.

Assessors perform the same duties as appraisers and then compute the amount of tax to be levied on property, using applicable tax tables. The primary responsibility of the assessor is to prepare an annual assessment roll, which lists all properties in a district and their assessed values.

To prepare the assessment roll, assessors and their staffs first must locate and identify all taxable property in the district. To do so, they prepare and maintain complete and accurate maps that show the size, shape, location, and legal description of each parcel of land. Next, they collect information about other features, such as zoning, soil characteristics, and availability of water, electricity, sewers, gas, and telephones. They describe each building and how land and buildings are used. This information is put in a parcel record.

Assessors also analyze relationships between property characteristics and sales prices, rents, and construction costs to produce valuation models or formulas. They use these formulas to estimate the value of every property as of the legally required assessment date. For example, assessors try to estimate the value of adding a bedroom to a residence or adding an acre to a farm, or how much competition from a new shopping center detracts from the value of a downtown department store. Finally, assessors prepare and certify an assessment roll listing all properties, owners, and assessed values and notify owners of the assessed value of their properties. Because taxpayers have the right to contest their assessments, assessors must be prepared to defend their estimates and methods.

Personal property assessors help the government levy taxes by preparing lists of personal property owned by businesses and, in a

An appraiser (left) tells a woman and her family about the history of a clock they have brought to an antique show. (Kathy McLaughlin, The Image Works)

few areas, householders. In addition to listing the number of items, these assessors also estimate the value of taxable items.

REQUIREMENTS

High School

If you are interested in the fields of assessing or appraising, there are a number of courses you can take in high school to help prepare you for this work. Take plenty of math classes, since you will need to be comfortable working with numbers and making calculations. Accounting classes will also be helpful for the same reasons. English courses will help you develop your researching and writing skills as well as verbal skills. Take computer classes in order to become accustomed to using this tool. Courses in civics or government may also be beneficial.

Postsecondary Training

Appraisers and assessors need a broad range of knowledge in such areas as equity and mortgage finance, architectural function, demographic statistics, and business trends. In addition, they must be competent writers and able to communicate effectively with people. In the past, some people have been able to enter these fields with only a high school education and learn specialized skills on the job. Today, however, most appraisers and assessors have at least some college education. A number work in appropriate businesses, such as auction houses, while they earn their degrees. Some with several years of college experience are able to find employment and receive on-the-job training. Those wanting to receive professional designations and to have the best job opportunities, however, should complete a college degree.

A few colleges and universities, such as Lindenwood University (http://www.lindenwood.edu) in St. Charles, Missouri, now offer degrees in valuation sciences that will prepare you for this career. If you are unable to attend such a specialized program, though, there are numerous classes you can take at any college to prepare for this career. A liberal arts degree provides a solid background, as do courses in finance, statistics, mathematics, public administration and business administration, real estate and urban land economics, engineering, architecture, and computer science. Appraisers choosing to specialize in a particular area should have a solid background in that field.

Courses in assessment and appraisal are offered by professional associations such as the American Society of Appraisers (ASA), the Appraisal Institute (AI), and the International Association of Assessing Officers.

Certification or Licensing

A number of professional organizations, such as the ASA and the AI, offer certification or designations in the field. It is highly recommended that you attain professional designation in order to enhance your standing in the field and demonstrate to consumers your level of expertise. To receive a designation, you will typically need to pass a written exam, demonstrate ethical behavior, and have completed a certain amount of education. To maintain your designation, you will also need to fulfill continuing education requirements.

Because all appraisals used for federally regulated real estate transactions must be conducted by licensed appraisers, most appraisers now obtain a state license. In addition, some states—known as "mandatory states"—require real estate appraisers to be licensed even if the appraisers do not deal with federally regulated transactions. You will need to check with your state's regulatory agency to learn more about the exact requirements for your state. In addition to a license, some states may require assessors who are government employees to pass civil service tests or other examinations before they can start work.

Other Requirements

Good appraisers are skilled investigators and must be proficient at gathering data. They must be familiar with sources of information on such diverse topics as public records, construction materials, building trends, economic trends, and governmental regulations affecting use of property. They should know how to read survey drawings and blueprints and be able to identify features of building construction.

EXPLORING

One simple way you can practice the methods used by appraisers is to write a detailed analysis of something you are considering investing in, such as a car, a computer, or even which college to attend. Your analysis should include both the benefits and the shortcomings of the investment as well as your final recommendation. Is the car overpriced? Does one particular school offer a better value for you? By doing this, you will begin to get a feel for the researching and writing done by an appraiser. Another way to explore this career is to look for part-time or summer work with an appraisal firm. Some firms also have jobs as appraiser assistants or trainees. Working at county assessors' or treasurers' offices, financial institutions, or real estate companies also might provide experience. If you are interested in working with real estate, you may want to learn the particulars of building construction by finding summer work with a construction company.

EMPLOYERS

Assessors are public servants who are either elected or appointed to office. The United States is divided into assessment districts, with population size affecting the number of assessors in a given area. Appraisers are employed by private businesses, such as accounting firms, real estate companies, and financial institutions, and by larger assessors' offices. Appraisers also work at auction houses, art galleries, and antique shops; some also work in government offices or for U.S. Customs and Border Protection. Assessors' offices might employ administrators, property appraisers, mappers, systems analysts, computer technicians, public relations specialists, word processors, and clerical workers. In small offices, one or two people might handle most tasks; in large offices, some with hundreds of employees, specialists are more common. Approximately 102,000 real estate assessors and appraisers are employed in the United States.

STARTING OUT

After you have acquired the necessary technical and mathematical knowledge in the classroom, you should apply to area appraisal firms, local county assessors, real estate brokers, or large accounting firms. Because assessing jobs are often civil service positions, they may be listed with government employment agencies. If you have graduated from a degree program in valuation sciences, your school's career services office should also be able to provide you with assistance in finding that first job.

ADVANCEMENT

Appraising is a dynamic field, affected yearly by new legislation and technology. To distinguish themselves in the business, top appraisers continue their education and pursue certification through the various national appraising organizations, such as the Appraisal Institute, the American Society of Appraisers, and the International Association of Assessing Officers. Certified appraisers are entrusted with the most prestigious projects and can command the highest fees. In addition to working on more and more prestigious projects, some appraisers advance by opening their own appraisal firms. Others may advance by moving to larger firms or agency offices, where they are more able to specialize.

EARNINGS

Income for assessors is influenced by their location and employer; their salaries generally increase as the population of their jurisdiction increases. For example, those working in large counties, such as Los Angeles County, may make up to $100,000 annually. Appraisers employed in the private sector tend to earn higher incomes than those in the public sector.

According to a recent survey by *Appraisal Today,* the average annual income of all appraisers is $58,132. Salaries range from $12,500 to $225,000.

The average fee for appraisal of a standard residential property is about $300, but fees can range from $75 for a re-inspection of new construction or repairs to $600 for inspection of a small residential income property.

According to the U.S. Department of Labor, real estate appraisers and assessors earned a median salary of $44,460 in 2006. The lowest paid 10 percent earned $24,000 or less per year on average, while the highest paid earned $86,140 or more.

Earnings at any level are enhanced by higher education and professional designations. Fringe benefits for both public and private employees usually include paid vacations and health insurance.

WORK ENVIRONMENT

Appraisers and assessors have a variety of working conditions, from the comfortable offices where they write and edit appraisal reports to outdoor construction sites, which they visit in both the heat of summer and the bitter cold of winter. Many appraisers spend mornings at their desks and afternoons in the field. Experienced appraisers may need to travel out of state.

Appraisers and assessors who work for a government agency or financial institution usually work 40-hour weeks, with overtime when necessary. Independent appraisers often can set their own schedules.

Appraisal is a very people-oriented occupation. Appraisers must be unfailingly cordial, and they have to deal calmly and tactfully with people who challenge their decisions (and are usually angry). Appraising can be a high-stress occupation because a considerable amount of money and important personal decisions ride on appraisers' calculations.

OUTLOOK

The U.S. Department of Labor estimates that employment of assessors and appraisers will grow faster than the average for all occupations through 2014 due to increases in real estate sales. In general, assessors work in a fairly secure field. As long as governments levy property taxes, assessors will be needed to provide them with information. The real estate industry, however, is influenced dramatically by the overall health of the economy, so appraisers in real estate can expect to benefit during periods of growth and experience slowdowns during recessions and depressions.

FOR MORE INFORMATION

For information on education and professional designations, contact
American Society of Appraisers
555 Herndon Parkway, Suite 125
Herndon, VA 20170-5250
Tel: 703-478-2228

Email: asainfo@appraisers.org
http://www.appraisers.org

Visit this organization's Web site for a listing of state real estate appraiser regulatory boards.
The Appraisal Foundation
1155 15th Street, NW, Suite 1111
Washington, DC 20005-2706
Tel: 202-347-7722
Email: info@appraisalfoundation.org
http://www.appraisalfoundation.org

For information on professional designations, education, careers, and scholarships, contact
Appraisal Institute
550 West Van Buren Street, Suite 1000
Chicago, IL 60607-3805
Tel: 312-335-4100
http://www.appraisalinstitute.org

For information on professional designations, education, and publications, contact
International Association of Assessing Officers
314 West 10th Street
Kansas City, MO 64105-1616
Tel: 816-701-8100
http://www.iaao.org

For information on education and appraisal careers, contact
National Association of Independent Fee Appraisers
401 North Michigan Avenue, Suite 2200
Chicago, IL 60611-4245
Tel: 312-321-6830
Email: info@naifa.com
http://www.naifa.com

For information on jewelry appraising, contact
National Association of Jewelry Appraisers
PO Box 18
Rego Park, NY 11374-0018
Tel: 718-896-1536
Email: naja.appraisers@netzero.net
http://www.najaappraisers.com

INTERVIEW

Arthur Skuratowicz and Julie Nash are the owners of Anton Nash LLC, an independent jewelry appraisal company, as well as the authors of Working With Gemstones: A Bench Jeweler's Guide. *They discussed their careers with the editors of* Careers in Focus: Mathematics and Physics.

Q. Please tell us about your business.

A. We currently own Anton Nash, LLC, which is an independent jewelry appraisal and consulting firm. By "independent" we mean that we are not in the business of buying or selling jewelry—just appraising. Both of us worked in upscale retail stores before forming Anton Nash.

Q. Please tell us about your professional backgrounds.

A. (Arthur): I am a third-generation jeweler who grew up in the family business and was the first teacher at the Gemological Institute of America (GIA) to teach both gemology and jewelry manufacturing. I am also an independent certified gemologist appraiser with the American Gem Society, a senior member of the National Association of Jewelry Appraisers, and hold the graduate jeweler gemologist diploma from the GIA.

(Julie): I started as a silversmith and designer and taught at the GIA. I am a certified gemologist with the American Gem Society, as well as an accredited senior appraiser and master gemologist appraiser with the American Society of Appraisers.

Q. Please tell us about your new venture, the Jewelry Training Center.

A. Part of our responsibilities include traveling and teaching for various organizations like Jewelers of America, the GIA, Platinum Guild International, and the Manufacturing Jewelers and Suppliers of America (MJSA). The MJSA is also the publisher of our book. The Jewelry Training Center (JTC) is a permanent school in Colorado Springs, Colorado, where we use our teaching experience. The JTC is in a user-friendly community where students can concentrate on learning bench skills, design, gemology, and the ins and outs of customer relationships in the jewelry business.

Q. What are some of the pros and cons of your job?

A. As appraisers we work directly with the public and get to hear (and see) both the positive and negative in their experience with jewelers and jewelry. The pros of the job are meeting varied and interesting people, seeing some fantastic jewelry, and seeing firsthand a consumer's pride in a jewelry purchase. The cons are being the bearers of bad news about jewelry, having to tell someone that their new diamond ring has cracked prongs and loose stones, or that the diamond that they purchased as "perfect" is in fact low clarity and color as well as badly cut. This gives us a deep sense of embarrassment for our industry and strongly proves the need for technical training for both bench jewelers and sales associates.

Q. What advice would you give to young people who are interested in entering this field?

A. Learn, learn, learn! Work, work, work. Gain work experience. Learn what to do or what not to do. This experience will temper you for a career in jewelry. Formal education is important, too, so seek it out. Network with established jewelers who can share knowledge and techniques. Read books and magazines about technique and design. Learn about the gemological properties of gemstones so that you can handle them safely. Try new techniques and experiment to expand techniques.

Astronomers

QUICK FACTS

School Subjects
Mathematics
Physics

Personal Skills
Communication/ideas
Technical/scientific

Work Environment
Primarily indoors
Primarily one location

Minimum Education Level
Bachelor's degree

Salary Range
$44,590 to $95,740 to
$145,600+

Certification or Licensing
None available

Outlook
More slowly than the average

DOT
021

GOE
02.02.01

NOC
2111

O*NET-SOC
19-2011.00

OVERVIEW

Astronomers study the universe and its celestial bodies by collecting and analyzing data. They also compute positions of stars and planets and calculate orbits of comets, asteroids, and artificial satellites. Astronomers make statistical studies of stars and galaxies and prepare mathematical tables giving positions of the sun, moon, planets, and stars at a given time. They study the size and shape of the earth and the properties of its upper atmosphere through observation and through data collected by spacecraft and earth satellites. There are approximately 1,400 astronomers employed in the United States.

HISTORY

The term *astronomy* is derived from two Greek words: *astron*, meaning star, and *nemein*, meaning to arrange or distribute. It is one of the oldest sciences. The field has historically attracted people who have a natural fascination with our universe. Astronomers have traditionally been driven by a desire to learn; the pursuit of practical applications of astronomy has, for many, been secondary.

One of the earliest practical applications, the establishment of a calendar based on celestial movement, was pursued by many ancient civilizations, including the Babylonians, Chinese, Mayans, Europeans, and Egyptians. A chief aim of early astronomers was to study the motion of the bodies in the sky in order to create a calendar that could be used to predict certain celestial events and provide a more orderly structure to social life. The ancient Babylonians were among the first to construct a calendar based on the movement of the sun and the phases of the moon;

46

their calendar has been found to have been accurate within minutes. In Europe, stone mounds constructed by ancient inhabitants also attest to astronomical work. Stonehenge is one of the largest and most famous of these mounds.

Ancient Greek astronomers introduced a new concept of astronomy by attempting to identify the physical structure of the universe, a branch of astronomy that has become known as *cosmology*. Astronomers such as Aristotle, Apollonius, Hipparchus, and Ptolemy succeeded in describing the universe in terms of circular movements. Their discoveries and theories were adopted by astronomers throughout much of the world. Modern astronomy was born with the theory of the sun-centered universe, first proposed by Nicolaus Copernicus in the 16th century. Copernicus's discovery revolutionized the field of astronomy and later would have a dramatic impact on many aspects of science.

After thousands of years, astronomers had succeeded in developing accurate predictions of celestial events. Next, they turned to newly evolving areas of astronomy, those of identifying the structure of the universe and of understanding the physical nature of the bodies they observed. Astronomers were aided by the invention of telescopes, and, as these increased in power, astronomers began to make new discoveries in the skies. For much of history, for example, it was believed that there were only five planets in the solar system. By the end of the 17th century, that number had increased to six, and, over the next two centuries, three more planets—Neptune, Uranus, and Pluto—were discovered. (In 2006, Pluto was downgraded to "dwarf planet" status by the International Astronomical Union.)

Astronomers have always relied heavily on tools to bring faraway worlds close enough for study. As technology has evolved, so then has the field of astronomy. Spectroscopy, invented in the 19th century, allowed astronomers to identify the elements that make up the composition of the planets and other celestial bodies and gave rise to a new branch of astronomy, called *astrophysics*, which describes the components of the universe by measuring such information as temperature, chemical composition, pressure, and density. Later, photography, too, became an important research aid. In the early 20th century, new discoveries further revolutionized the field of astronomy, particularly with the discovery of other galaxies beyond our own. The understanding grew that the universe was constructed of many millions of galaxies, each an island in an infiniteness of space.

By the middle of the 20th century, scientists had learned how to send rockets, and later manned spacecraft, into space to gain a closer view of the universe surrounding us. Using satellites and unmanned space probes, astronomers have been able to travel far into the solar system, toward the most distant planets. A major event in astronomy occurred with the launching in 1990 of the powerful Hubble Space Telescope, which orbits the earth and continues to send back information and photographs of events and phenomena across the universe.

THE JOB

Astronomers study the universe and all of its celestial bodies. They collect and analyze information about the moon, planets, sun, and stars, which they use to predict their shapes, sizes, brightness, and motions.

They are interested in the orbits of comets, asteroids, and even artificial satellites. Information on the size and shape, the luminosity and position, the composition, characteristics, and structure as well as temperature, distance, motion, and orbit of all celestial bodies is of great relevance to their work.

Practical application of activity in space is used for a variety of purposes. The launching of space vehicles and satellites has increased the importance of the information astronomers gather. For example, the public couldn't enjoy the benefits of accurate weather prediction if satellites weren't keeping an eye on our atmosphere. Without astronomical data, satellite placement wouldn't be possible. Knowledge of the orbits of planets and their moons, as well as asteroid activity, is also vital to astronauts exploring space.

Astronomers are usually expected to specialize in some particular branch of astronomy. The *astrophysicist* is concerned with applying the concepts of physics to stellar atmospheres and interiors. *Radio astronomers* study the source and nature of celestial radio waves with extremely sensitive radio telescopes. The majority of astronomers either teach or do research or a combination of both. Astronomers in many universities are expected to teach such subjects as physics and mathematics in addition to astronomy. Other astronomers are engaged in such activities as the development of astronomical instruments, administration, technical writing, and consulting.

Astronomers who make observations may spend long periods of time in observatories. Astronomers who teach or work in laboratories may work eight-hour days. However, those who make observations, especially during celestial events or other peak viewing times, may spend long evening hours in observatories. Paperwork is a necessary part of the job. For teachers, it can include lesson planning

An astronomy professor takes notes as his student uses a telescope to view a planetary nebula. *(Alan Carey, The Image Works)*

and paper grading. Astronomers conducting research independently or for a university can expect to spend a considerable amount of time writing grant proposals to secure funding for their work. For any scientist, sharing the knowledge acquired is a vital part of the work. Astronomers are expected to painstakingly document their observations and eventually combine them into a coherent report, often for peer review or publication.

Although the telescope is the major instrument used in observation, many other devices are also used by astronomers in carrying out these studies, including spectrometers for the measurement of wavelengths of radiant energy, photometers for the measurement of light intensity, balloons for carrying various measuring devices, and computers for processing and analyzing all the information gathered.

Astronomers use ground-based telescopes for night observation of the skies. The Hubble Space Telescope (http://hubblesite.org), which magnifies the stars at a much greater percentage than land-based capability allows, has become an important tool for the work of many astronomers.

REQUIREMENTS

High School

While in high school, prospective astronomers should take mathematics (including analytical geometry and trigonometry), science courses (including chemistry and physics), English, foreign languages, and courses in the humanities and social sciences. Students should also be well grounded in the use of computers and in computer programming.

Postsecondary Training

All astronomers are required to have some postsecondary training, with a doctoral degree being the usual educational requirement because most jobs are in research and development. A master's degree is sufficient for some jobs in applied research and development, and a bachelor's degree is adequate for some nonresearch jobs. Students should select a college program with wide offerings in physics, mathematics, and astronomy and take as many of these courses as possible. Graduate training will normally take at least three years beyond the bachelor's degree.

Bachelor's degrees in astronomy are offered by about 80 institutions in the United States, and 40 institutions offer master's degrees or doctorates in the field, often combined with physics departments. Some of the astronomy courses typically offered in graduate school are celestial mechanics, galactic structure, radio astronomy, stellar atmospheres and interiors, theoretical astrophysics, and binary and variable stars. Some graduate schools require that an applicant for a doctorate spend several months in residence at an observatory. In most institutions the student's graduate courses will reflect his or her chosen astronomical specialty or particular field of interest.

Other Requirements

The field of astronomy calls for people with a strong but controlled imagination. They must be able to see relationships between what may appear to be, on the surface, unrelated facts, and they must be able to form various hypotheses regarding these relationships. Astronomers must be able to concentrate over long periods of time. They should also express themselves well in both writing and verbally.

EXPLORING

A number of summer or part-time jobs are usually available in observatories. The latter may be either on a summer or year-round basis. These jobs not only offer experience in astronomy but often act as stepping stones to good jobs upon graduation. Students employed in observatories might work as guides or as assistants to astronomers.

Students can test their interest in this field by working part time, either as an employee or as a volunteer, in planetariums or science museums. Many people enjoy astronomy as a hobby, and there are a number of amateur astronomy clubs and groups active throughout the country. Amateur astronomers have often made important contributions to the field of astronomy. In 1996, for example, a new comet was discovered by an amateur astronomer in Japan. Students may gain experience in studying the skies by purchasing, or even building, their own telescopes.

Reading or using the Internet to learn more on your own is also a good idea. What about astronomy interests you? You can find specific information in books or on the Internet. Check out NASA's Web site at http://www.nasa.gov. It contains useful information about careers in astronomy and aeronautics and information about current space exploration. Another interesting Web site is http://www.absoluteastronomy.com, which contains information on planets, constellations, nebulas, galaxies, and other topics. When you hear in the news that a comet or meteor shower will be visible from Earth, be sure to set your alarm to get up and watch and learn. Science teachers will often discuss such events in class.

EMPLOYERS

Approximately one-third of all physicists and astronomers work for scientific research and development companies. Another 25 percent work for the federal government. Astronomers represent only a small portion of these workers. The federal government employs astronomers in agencies such as NASA, the U.S. Naval Observatory, the U.S. Department of Defense, and the Naval Research Laboratory.

Astronomers more frequently find jobs as faculty members at colleges and universities or are affiliated with those institutions through observatories and laboratories. Other astronomers work in planetariums, in science museums, or in other public service positions involved in presenting astronomy to the general public; others teach physics or earth sciences in secondary schools or are science journalists and writers.

In the private sector, astronomers are hired by consulting firms that supply astronomical talent to the government for specific tasks. In addition, a number of companies in the aerospace industry hire astronomers to work in related areas in order to use their background and talents in instrumentation, remote sensing, spectral observations, and computer applications.

STARTING OUT

A chief method of entry for astronomers with a doctorate is to register with the college's career services office, which provides contacts with one of the agencies looking for astronomers. Astronomers can also apply directly to universities, colleges, planetariums, government agencies, aerospace industry manufacturers, and others who hire astronomers. Many positions are advertised in professional and scientific journals devoted to astronomy and astrophysics.

Graduates with bachelor's or master's degrees can normally obtain semiprofessional positions in observatories, planetariums, or some of the larger colleges and universities offering training in astronomy. Their work assignments might be as research assistants, optical workers, observers, or technical assistants. Those employed by colleges or universities might well begin as instructors. Federal government positions in astronomy are usually earned on the basis of competitive examinations. Jobs with some municipal organizations employing astronomers are often based on competitive examinations. The examinations are usually open to those with bachelor's degrees.

NASA offers internships for students with some postsecondary training. To find out more about NASA internships and other opportunities, explore its Web site, http://www.nasajobs.nasa.gov.

ADVANCEMENT

Because of the relatively small size of the field, advancement may be somewhat limited. A professional position in a large university or governmental agency is often considered the most desirable post available to an astronomer because of the opportunities it offers for additional study and research. Those employed in colleges may well advance from instructor to assistant professor to associate professor and then to professor. There is also the possibility of eventually becoming a department head.

Opportunities also exist for advancement in observatories or industries employing people in astronomy. In these situations, as in those in colleges and universities, advancement depends to a great extent on the astronomer's ability, education, and experience. Peer recognition, in particular for discoveries that broaden the understanding of the field, is often a determinant of advancement. Publishing articles in professional journals, such as *Scientific American* or the *Journal of Astrophysics and Astronomy,* is a way for astronomers to become known and respected in the field. Advancement isn't usually speedy; an astronomer may spend years devoted to a specific research problem before being able to publish conclusions or discoveries in a scientific journal.

EARNINGS

According to the U.S. Department of Labor, astronomers had median annual earnings of $95,740 in 2006. Salaries ranged from less than $44,590 to $145,600 or more annually. The average for astronomers employed by the federal government in 2006 was $117,350, according to the U.S. Department of Labor.

In educational institutions, salaries are normally regulated by the salary schedule prevailing in that particular institution. As the astronomer advances to higher-level teaching positions, his or her salary increases significantly.

Opportunities also exist in private industry for well-trained and experienced astronomers, who often find their services in demand as consultants. Fees for this type of work may run as high as $200 per day in some of the more specialized fields of astronomy.

WORK ENVIRONMENT

Astronomers' activities may center on the optical telescope. Most telescopes are located high on a hill or mountain and normally in a fairly remote area, where the air is clean and the view is not affected by lights from unrelated sources. There are approximately 300 of these observatories in the United States.

Astronomers working in these observatories usually are assigned to observation from three to six nights per month and spend the remainder of their time in an office or laboratory, where they study and analyze their data. They also must prepare reports. They may work with others on one segment of their research or writing and then work entirely alone on the next. Their work is normally carried on in clean, quiet, well-ventilated, and well-lighted facilities.

Those astronomers in administrative positions, such as director of an observatory or planetarium, will maintain fairly steady office hours but may also work during the evening and night. They usually are more involved in administrative details, however, spending less time in observation and research.

Those employed as teachers will usually have good facilities available to them, and their hours will vary according to class hours assigned. Astronomers who are employed by colleges and universities may often work more than 40 hours per week.

OUTLOOK

Employment for astronomers will grow more slowly than the average for all occupations through 2014, according to the U.S. Department of Labor. Astronomy is one of the smallest science fields. Job openings result from the normal turnover when workers retire or leave the field for other reasons. Competition for these jobs, particularly among new people entering the profession, will continue to be strong. In recent years, the number of new openings in this field have not kept pace with the number of astronomers graduating from the universities, and this trend is likely to continue for the near future. Furthermore, there will likely be few new positions made, since funding in this area is hard to come by.

The federal government will continue to provide employment opportunities for astronomers. Defense expenditures are expected to increase over the next decade, and this should provide stronger employment opportunities for astronomers who work on defense-related research projects. However, government agencies, particularly NASA, may find their budgets reduced in the coming years, and the number of new positions created for astronomers will likely drop as well. Few new observatories will be constructed, and those currently in existence are not expected to greatly increase the size of their staffs.

The greatest growth in employment of astronomers is expected to occur in business and industry. Companies in the aerospace field will need more astronomers to do research to help them develop new equipment and technology.

FOR MORE INFORMATION

Visit the FAQ section of this association's Web site to read the online article Career Profile: Astronomy.
American Association of Amateur Astronomers
PO Box 7981
Dallas, TX 75209-0981
Email: aaaa@astromax.com
http://www.astromax.com

To read A New Universe to Discover: A Guide to Careers in Astronomy, visit the AAS Web site.
American Astronomical Society (AAS)
2000 Florida Avenue, NW, Suite 400
Washington, DC 20009-1231
Tel: 202-328-2010
Email: aas@aas.org
http://www.aas.org

For a list of print and online resources about astronomy, contact
Astronomical Society of the Pacific
390 Ashton Avenue
San Francisco, CA 94112-1722
Tel: 415-337-1100
http://www.astrosociety.org

This organization is a resource for professionals who work in many physics disciplines, including astronomy. For more information, contact
American Institute of Physics
One Physics Ellipse
College Park, MD 20740-3843
Tel: 301-209-3100
http://www.aip.org

Astrophysicists

QUICK FACTS

School Subjects
Mathematics
Physics

Personal Skills
Communication/ideas
Technical/scientific

Work Environment
Primarily indoors
Primarily one location

Minimum Education Level
Bachelor's degree

Salary Range
$52,070 to $94,240 to
$143,570+

Certification or Licensing
None available

Outlook
More slowly than the average

DOT
023

GOE
02.02.01

NOC
2111

O*NET-SOC
19-2011.00, 19-2012.00

OVERVIEW

Astrophysics is a specialty that combines two fields of science: astronomy and physics. *Astrophysicists* use the principles of physics to study the solar system, stars, galaxies, and the universe. How did the universe begin? How is the universe changing? These are the types of questions astrophysicists try to answer through research and experimentation. Physicists may also be concerned with such issues, but they use physics to study broader areas such as gravity, electromagnetism, and nuclear interactions.

HISTORY

Astrophysics began in the 1800s, when astronomers developed the spectroscope, which is used to determine the various properties of stars and planets. In spectroscopy, light is spread into a spectrum, and the resulting image can be used to determine a star's chemical composition, temperature, surface condition, and other properties. Astrophysicists knew that understanding the nature of stars would help them understand the larger question that all astrophysicists work toward answering: How did the universe begin?

A major advance in the field of astrophysics was the development of atomic theory. In 1803, a British chemist, John Dalton, proposed that each natural element consists of a particular kind of atom. In the early 1900s, scientists discovered that each atom has a nucleus, which contains protons, neutrons, and electrons that interact with each other. Today the atom is the basis of the study of physics. Physicists of all disciplines, from astrophysicists to nuclear physicists, use what we know about the atom and its parts to understand their respective fields.

In the case of astrophysicists, close examination of the parts of the atom will help to understand how matter and our universe formed. A widely held explanation today is the "Big Bang" theory, which hypothesizes that the universe was formed 15 to 20 billion years ago when a dense singular point of matter exploded and eventually formed stars and galaxies. Today most astrophysicists believe the universe is still expanding from that initial explosion.

THE JOB

To do their work, astrophysicists need access to large, expensive equipment, such as radio telescopes, spectrometers, and specialized computers. This equipment is generally available only at universities with large astronomy departments and government observatories; therefore most astrophysicists are employed by colleges or the government.

A primary duty of most astrophysicists is making and recording observations. What they observe and the questions they are trying to answer may vary, but the process is much the same across the profession. They work in observatories, using telescopes and other equipment to view celestial bodies. They record their observations on charts or, more often today, into computer programs that help them analyze the data.

Astrophysicists work to understand the beginning and the end of the lives of stars. They use spectrometers, telescopes, and other instruments to measure infrared radiation, ultraviolet radiation, and radio waves. They study not only the formation of stars but also whether planets formed along with them. Understanding the lives of stars will help astrophysicists understand the origins and future of the universe. Their work is often tedious, requiring multiple measurements over time. The answer to one question, such as the age of a specific star, often leads to more questions about nearby planets and other formations. To address these larger questions, astrophysicists from all over the world must work together to come to agreements.

Most astrophysicists who work for universities also teach. Depending on their branch of research, teaching may be their primary duty. Astrophysicists share their findings with the scientific community. They often travel to conferences to speak about their findings and to listen to other scientists discuss techniques or research. Discoveries are also shared in professional journals, such as the *Astrophysical Journal*. Many scientists spend time compiling their data and writing articles for such journals.

Interesting Web Sites

Adler Planetarium
http://www.adlerplanetarium.org

Astronomy Basics
http://www.astronomybasics.com

Astronomy Now
http://www.astronomy-now.com

Jack Horkheimer: Star Gazer
http://www.jackstargazer.com

Hubble Space Telescope
http://hubble.nasa.gov/index.php

NASA's Imagine the Universe
http://imagine.gsfc.nasa.gov

Night Sky Info
http://www.nightskyinfo.com

A Practical Guide to Astronomy
http://www.hotliquidmagma.com/space/index.html

Yahoo: Astronomy
http://dir.yahoo.com/Science/astronomy

You Be the Astrophysicist!
http://imagine.gsfc.nasa.gov/YBA/yba-intro.html

REQUIREMENTS

High School

If you are interested in becoming an astrophysicist, concentrate on classes in mathematics and science. If they are available, take classes at an advanced level to better prepare for challenging college courses. English skills are also important because astrophysicists must write up their results, communicate with other scientists, and lecture on their findings. Finally, make sure you are comfortable working with computers either by taking a computer science class or by exploring on your own.

Postsecondary Training

An advanced degree is highly desirable for a career in astrophysics. A few who have bachelor's degrees in physics, astronomy, or mathematics may work as research assistants in the field. To do your own research or teach, you should have at least a master's degree, with a Ph.D. preferred for full astrophysicists.

Other Requirements

Because astrophysicists deal with abstract concepts and faraway celestial bodies, an active imagination and the ability to draw logical conclusions from observational data are helpful traits. Some research can be tedious and take long periods of time; astrophysicists must be patient in their work and have the ability to remain focused and meet deadlines.

Astrophysicists who have a natural curiosity about why things occur no doubt enjoy their work most when research or experiments culminate in a discovery that will help them and others in the field gain a larger understanding of the universe.

EMPLOYERS

Because astrophysicists require such expensive equipment to do their job, their employers are generally limited to large colleges or government agencies. Some government agencies that employ astrophysicists include the National Aeronautics and Space Administration (NASA), the U.S. Naval Observatory, and Fermi National Accelerator Laboratory, known as Fermilab, a physics laboratory. Fermilab is the home of the world's most powerful particle accelerator, which scientists from various institutions use to conduct research to better understand energy and the atom.

According to the U.S. Department of Labor, there are approximately 16,000 physicists and astronomers working in the United States. Most work for scientific research and development services firms. Approximately 25 percent work for the federal government, mostly with the Department of Defense and NASA. Others work for colleges or universities, either as faculty members or in nonfaculty research positions. These scientists work all over the country, but most are employed in areas where large universities or research laboratories are located.

STARTING OUT

Many astrophysicists get their first paying job as graduate students who assist professors in astronomy, physics, or astrophysics. These assistant jobs are known in the field as postdoctoral positions. Students may help the professors grade undergraduate and graduate papers or assist them in recording and compiling astronomical data in the observatory. Beginning jobs in government may include internships or temporary positions with specific research projects. The job market for astrophysicists is very competitive; students and recent graduates often must volunteer their time at university or government observatories and work other jobs until they can find full-time, paid work.

ADVANCEMENT

Astrophysicists work with other highly educated people, including mathematicians, astronomers, and other scientists. Astrophysicists who work for large universities or the government should have a sense of the "department politics" that may go on at their university and be able to deal diplomatically with department heads and colleagues competing for resources such as grants and equipment.

At the beginning of their careers, astrophysicists may be assigned to work nights at the observatory. Hours can be long and pay can be limited. After they have gained experience, astrophysicists can expect to be involved in the planning and development stages of research and may not be required to do as much observation and data recording. With further experience, astrophysicists can advance to become tenured professors, research institution leaders, or observatory managers.

EARNINGS

Salaries for astrophysicists tend to parallel those listed for astronomers and physicists because of their job similarities. According to the U.S. Department of Labor, the median annual salary of physicists was $94,240 in 2006. The lowest paid 10 percent earned less than $52,070, and the highest paid 10 percent earned over $143,570.

The American Institute of Physics reported the following median earnings for physicists by degree level in 2004: Ph.D.'s (excluding those in postdoctoral positions), $104,000; master's degrees, $94,000; and bachelor's degrees, $72,000.

WORK ENVIRONMENT

Astrophysicists generally work regular hours in laboratories, observatories, or classrooms. However, some research may require them to work extended or irregular hours. A research deadline or a celestial event such as a meteor shower or asteroid may require extra hours or overnight observation. Some travel may be required, such as to an observatory with a needed piece of equipment or to a conference or training. The astrophysicist's employer generally pays for the travel. Astrophysicists work with other highly educated professionals, such as mathematicians, astronomers, and other scientists. The work environment can be competitive and sometimes political because these professionals often compete for the same limited resources.

OUTLOOK

The outlook for astrophysics, because it is so closely related to astronomy and physics, mirrors the outlook for those fields. According to the U.S. Department of Labor, employment in these fields will grow slower than the average for all occupations through 2014. The need for scientists, especially those employed by the government, is affected by factors outside the field, such as budgetary cuts and political issues that draw attention (and funding) away from expensive research programs.

Aspiring astrophysicists should be prepared for a tight job market, especially in research positions. Within private industry, many companies are reducing their amount of basic research (which includes physics-related research) in favor of applied research and software development. Job openings for engineers and computer scientists will far outnumber those for physicists and astrophysicists.

FOR MORE INFORMATION

For additional information on the field of astronomy, contact
American Astronomical Society
2000 Florida Avenue, NW, Suite 400
Washington, DC 20009-1231
Tel: 202-328-2010
Email: aas@aas.org
http://www.aas.org

This is an organization for professionals who work in different areas of physics, including astrophysics. For more information, contact
American Institute of Physics
One Physics Ellipse
College Park, MD 20740-3843
Tel: 301-209-3100
http://www.aip.org

To read articles on astrophysics, visit
The Astrophysical Journal
http://www.journals.uchicago.edu/ApJ

Bookkeeping and Accounting Clerks

QUICK FACTS

School Subjects
Business
Computer science
Mathematics

Personal Skills
Following instructions
Technical/scientific

Work Environment
Primarily indoors
Primarily one location

Minimum Education Level
High school diploma

Salary Range
$19,760 to $30,560 to
$46,020+

Certification or Licensing
Voluntary

Outlook
More slowly than the average

DOT
216

GOE
09.03.01

NOC
1431

O*NET-SOC
43-3031.00

OVERVIEW

Bookkeeping and accounting clerks record financial transactions for government, business, and other organizations. They compute, classify, record, and verify numerical data in order to develop and maintain accurate financial records. There are more than two million bookkeeping, accounting, and auditing clerks employed in the United States.

HISTORY

The history of bookkeeping developed along with the growth of business and industrial enterprise. The first known records of bookkeeping date back to 2600 B.C., when the Babylonians used pointed sticks to mark accounts on clay slabs. By 3000 B.C., Middle Eastern and Egyptian cultures employed a system of numbers to record merchants' transactions of the grain and farm products that were distributed from storage warehouses. The growth of intricate trade systems brought about the necessity for bookkeeping systems.

Sometime after the start of the 13th century, the decimal numeration system was introduced in Europe, simplifying bookkeeping record systems. The merchants of Venice—one of the busiest trading centers in the world at that time—are credited with the invention of the double entry bookkeeping method that is widely used today.

As industry in the United States expands and grows more complex, simpler and quicker bookkeeping methods and procedures

A bookkeeping clerk sorts through stacks of documents. *(Tony Savino, The Image Works)*

have evolved. Technological developments include bookkeeping machines, computer hardware and software, and electronic data processing.

THE JOB

Bookkeeping workers keep systematic records and current accounts of financial transactions for businesses, institutions, industries, charities, and other organizations. The bookkeeping records of a firm or business are a vital part of its operational procedures because these records reflect the assets and the liabilities, as well as the profits and losses, of the operation.

Bookkeepers record these business transactions daily in spreadsheets on computer databases, and accounting clerks often input the information. The practice of posting accounting records directly onto ledger sheets, in journals, or on other types of written accounting forms is decreasing as computerized record keeping becomes more widespread. In small businesses, bookkeepers sort and record all the sales slips, bills, check stubs, inventory lists, and requisition lists. They compile figures for cash receipts, accounts payable and receivable, and profits and losses.

Accounting clerks handle the clerical accounting work; they enter and verify transaction data and compute and record various charges. They may also monitor loans and accounts payable and receivable. More advanced clerks may reconcile billing vouchers, while senior workers review invoices and statements.

Accountants set up bookkeeping systems and use bookkeepers' balance sheets to prepare periodic summary statements of financial transactions. Management relies heavily on these bookkeeping records to interpret the organization's overall performance and uses them to make important business decisions. The records are also necessary to file income tax reports and prepare quarterly reports for stockholders.

Bookkeeping and accounting clerks work in retail and wholesale businesses, manufacturing firms, hospitals, schools, charities, and other types of institutional agencies. Many clerks are classified as financial institution bookkeeping and accounting clerks, insurance firm bookkeeping and accounting clerks, hotel bookkeeping and accounting clerks, and railroad bookkeeping and accounting clerks.

General bookkeepers and general-ledger bookkeepers are usually employed in smaller business operations. They may perform all the analysis, maintain the financial records, and complete any other tasks that are involved in keeping a full set of bookkeeping records. These employees may have other general office duties, such as mailing statements, answering telephone calls, and filing materials. Audit clerks verify figures and may be responsible for sending them on to an audit clerk supervisor.

In large companies, an accountant may supervise a department of bookkeepers who perform more specialized work. *Billing and rate clerks* and *fixed capital clerks* may post items in accounts payable or receivable ledgers, make out bills and invoices, or verify the company's rates for certain products and services. *Account information clerks* prepare reports, compile payroll lists and deductions, write company checks, and compute federal tax reports or personnel profit shares. Large companies may employ workers to organize, record, and compute many other types of financial information.

In large business organizations, bookkeepers and accountants may be classified by grades, such as Bookkeeper I or II. The job classification determines their responsibilities.

REQUIREMENTS

High School

In order to be a bookkeeper, you will need at least a high school diploma. It will be helpful to have a background in business mathematics, business writing, typing, and computer training. Pay particular attention to developing sound English and communication skills along with mathematical abilities.

Postsecondary Training

Some employers prefer people who have completed a junior college curriculum or those who have attended a postsecondary business training program. In many instances, employers offer on-the-job training for various types of entry-level positions. In some areas, work-study programs are available in which schools, in cooperation with businesses, offer part-time, practical on-the-job training combined with academic study. These programs often help students find immediate employment in similar work after graduation. Local business schools may also offer evening courses.

Certification or Licensing

The American Institute of Professional Bookkeepers offers voluntary certification to bookkeepers who have at least two years of full-time experience (or the part-time or freelance equivalent), pass an examination, and sign a code of ethics. Bookkeepers who complete this requirement may use the designation certified bookkeeper.

Other Requirements

Bookkeepers need strong mathematical skills and organizational abilities, and they have to be able to concentrate on detailed work.

The work is quite sedentary and often tedious, and you should not mind long hours behind a desk. You should be methodical, accurate, and orderly and enjoy working on detailed tasks. Employers look for honest, discreet, and trustworthy individuals when placing their business in someone else's hands.

Once you are employed as a bookkeeping and accounting clerk, some places of business may require you to have union membership. Larger unions include the Office and Professional Employees International Union; the International Union of Electronic, Electrical, Salaried, Machine, and Furniture Workers–Communications Workers of America; and the American Federation of State, County, and Municipal Employees. Also, depending on the business, clerks may be represented by the same union as other manufacturing employees.

EXPLORING

You can gain experience in bookkeeping by participating in work-study programs or by obtaining part-time or summer work in beginning bookkeeping jobs or related office work. Any retail experience dealing with cash management, pricing, or customer service is also valuable.

You can also volunteer to manage the books for extracurricular student groups. Managing income or cash flow for a club or acting as treasurer for student government are excellent ways to gain experience in maintaining financial records.

Other options are visiting local small businesses to observe their work and talking to representatives of schools that offer business training courses.

EMPLOYERS

Many of the more than two million bookkeeping, auditing, and accounting clerks in the United States work for employment services firms; that is, those companies that provide part-time or temporary office workers. Approximately 25 percent of bookkeeping and accounting clerks work part time, according to the U.S. Department of Labor. Many others are employed by government agencies and organizations that provide educational, health, business, and social services.

STARTING OUT

You may find jobs or establish contacts with businesses that are interested in interviewing graduates through your college's guidance or career services offices. A work-study program or internship may result in a full-time job offer. Business schools and junior colleges generally provide assistance to their graduates in locating employment.

You may locate job opportunities by applying directly to firms or responding to ads in newspaper classified sections. State employment agencies and private employment bureaus can also assist in the job search process.

ADVANCEMENT

Bookkeeping workers generally begin their employment by performing routine tasks, such as the simple recording of transactions. Beginners may start as entry-level clerks, cashiers, bookkeeping machine operators, office assistants, or typists. With experience, they may advance to more complex assignments that include computer training in databases and spreadsheets and assume a greater responsibility for the work as a whole.

With experience and education, clerks become department heads or office managers. Further advancement to positions such as office or division manager, department head, accountant, or auditor is possible with a college degree and years of experience. There is a high turnover rate in this field, which increases the promotion opportunities for employees with ability and initiative.

EARNINGS

According to the U.S. Department of Labor, bookkeepers and accounting clerks earned a median income of $30,560 a year in 2006. Earnings are also influenced by such factors as the size of the city where they work and the size and type of business for which they are employed. Clerks just starting out earn approximately $19,760 or less. Those with one or two years of college generally earn higher starting wages. Top-paying jobs average about $46,020 or more a year.

Employees usually receive six to eight paid holidays yearly and one week of paid vacation after six to 12 months of service. Paid vacations may increase to four weeks or more, depending on length of service and place of employment. Fringe benefits may include health and life insurance, sick leave, and retirement plans.

WORK ENVIRONMENT

The majority of office workers, including bookkeeping workers, usually work a 40-hour week, although some employees may work a 35- to 37-hour week. Bookkeeping and accounting clerks usually work in typical office settings. They are more likely to have a cubicle than an office. While the work pace is steady, it can also be routine and repetitive, especially in large companies where the employee is often assigned only one or two specialized job duties.

Attention to numerical details can be physically demanding, and the work can produce eyestrain and nervousness. While bookkeepers usually work with other people and sometimes under close supervision, they can expect to spend most of their day behind a desk; this may seem confining to people who need more variety and stimulation in their work. In addition, the constant attention to detail and the need for accuracy can place considerable responsibility on the worker and cause much stress.

OUTLOOK

Although the growing economy produces a demand for increased accounting services, the automation of office functions will continue to improve overall worker productivity. Fewer people will be needed to do the work, and employment of bookkeeping and accounting clerks is expected to grow more slowly than the average for all occupations through 2014, according to the U.S. Department of Labor. Excellent computer skills will be vital to securing a job.

Despite lack of growth, there will be numerous replacement job openings, since the turnover rate in this occupation is high. Offices are centralizing their operations, setting up one center to manage all accounting needs in a single location. As more companies trim back their workforces, opportunities for temporary work should continue to grow.

FOR MORE INFORMATION

For information on certification and career opportunities, contact
American Institute of Professional Bookkeepers
6001 Montrose Road, Suite 500
Rockville, MD 20852-4873
Tel: 800-622-0121
Email: info@aipb.org
http://www.aipb.org

For information on accredited educational programs, contact
The Association to Advance Collegiate Schools of Business
777 South Harbour Island Boulevard, Suite 750
Tampa, FL 33602-5730
Tel: 813-769-6500
http://www.aacsb.edu

For more information on women in accounting, contact
The Educational Foundation for Women in Accounting
PO Box 1925
Southeastern, PA 19399-1925
Tel: 610-407-9229
Email: info@efwa.org
http://www.efwa.org

Computer Systems Programmer/ Analysts

QUICK FACTS

School Subjects
Computer science
Mathematics

Personal Skills
Mechanical/manipulative
Technical/scientific

Work Environment
Primarily indoors
Primarily one location

Minimum Education Level
Bachelor's degree

Salary Range
$42,780 to $69,760 to
$106,820+

Certification or Licensing
Voluntary

Outlook
Much faster than the average

DOT
033

GOE
02.06.01

NOC
2162

O*NET-SOC
15-1051.00

OVERVIEW

Computer systems programmer/ analysts analyze the computing needs of a business and then design a new system or upgrade an old system to meet those needs. The position can be split between two people, the systems programmer and the systems analyst, but it is frequently held by just one person, who oversees the work from beginning to end.

HISTORY

The first major advances in modern computer technology were made during World War II. After the war, people thought that computers were too big (they easily filled entire warehouses) to ever be used for anything other than government projects, such as the processing of the 1950 census.

The introduction of semiconductors to computer technology led to the creation of smaller and less expensive computers. The semiconductors replaced the bigger, slower vacuum tubes of the first computers. These changes made it easier for businesses to adapt computers to their needs, which they began doing as early as 1954. Within 30 years, computers had revolutionized the way people work, play, and even shop. Today, computers are everywhere, from businesses of all kinds to government agencies, charitable organizations, and private homes. Over the years, technology has continued to shrink computer size and increase operating speeds at an unprecedented rate.

The need for systems programmer/analysts grew out of the proliferation of hardware and software products on the market. While many offices have an unofficial "computer expert," whose main job may be in accounting, word processing, or office administration, most medium-size to larger companies that have invested in expensive computer systems have found the need to employ, either full time or on a consulting basis, a systems analyst or programmer analyst.

In addition, the computer revolution brought with it awareness that choosing the appropriate system from the start is crucial to business success. Purchasing decisions are based on many complicated scientific and mathematical models as well as on practical business sense. Therefore, systems analysts have become essential to business decision-making.

Businesses and organizations also discovered that, like all new technology, computer systems break down a lot. It has become more cost effective for many organizations to have full-time systems analysts on site instead of calling computer repairers to fix every small glitch.

THE JOB

Businesses invest hundreds of thousands of dollars in computer systems to make their operations more efficient and thus, more profitable. As older systems become obsolete, businesses are also faced with the task of replacing them or upgrading them with new technology. Computer systems programmer/analysts plan and develop new computer systems or upgrade existing systems to meet changing business needs. They also install, modify, and maintain functioning computer systems. The process of choosing and implementing a computer system is similar for programmer analysts who work for very different employers. However, specific decisions in terms of hardware and software differ depending on the industry.

The first stage of the process involves meeting with management and users in order to discuss the problem at hand. For example, a company's accounting system might be slow, unreliable, and generally outdated. During many hours of meetings, systems programmer/analysts and management discuss various options, including commercial software, hardware upgrades, and customizing possibilities that may solve the problems. At the end of the discussions, which may last as long as several weeks or months, the programmer analyst defines the specific system goals as agreed upon by participants.

Next, systems programmer/analysts engage in highly analytic and logical activities. They use tools such as structural analysis, data modeling, mathematics, and cost accounting to determine which computers, including hardware and software and peripherals, will be required to meet the goals of the project. They must consider the trade-offs between extra efficiency and speed and increased costs. Weighing the pros and cons of each additional system feature is an important factor in system planning. Whatever preliminary decisions are made must be supported by mathematical and financial evidence.

As the final stage of the planning process, systems programmer/ analysts prepare reports and formal presentations to be delivered to management. Reports must be written in clear, concise language that business professionals, who are not necessarily technical experts, can understand thoroughly. Formal presentations in front of groups of various sizes are often required as part of the system proposal.

If the system or the system upgrades are approved, equipment is purchased and installed. Then, the programmer/analysts get down to the real technical work so that all the different computers and peripherals function well together. They prepare specifications, diagrams, and other programming structures and, often using computer-aided systems engineering (CASE) technology, they write the new or upgraded programming code. If they work solely as systems analysts, it is at this point that they hand over all of their information to the systems programmer so that he or she can begin to write the programming code.

Systems design and programming involves defining the files and records to be accessed by the system, outlining the processing steps, and suggesting formats for output that meet the needs of the company. User-friendliness of the front-end applications is extremely important for user productivity. Therefore, programmer/analysts must be able to envision how nontechnical system users view their on-screen work. Systems programmer/analysts might also specify security programs that allow only authorized personnel access to certain files or groups of files.

As the programs are written, programmer/analysts set up test runs of various parts of the system, making sure each step of the way that major goals are reached. Once the system is up and running, problems, or "bugs," begin to pop up. Programmer/analysts are responsible for fixing these last-minute problems. They must isolate the problem and review the hundreds of lines of programming commands to determine where the mistake is located. Then they must enter the correct command or code and recheck the program.

Depending on the employer, some systems programmer/analysts might be involved with computer networking. Network communi-

Books to Read

Frauenfelder, Mark. *Computers: An Illustrated History*. London, U.K.: Carlton Publishing Group, 2007.

Pasternak, Ceel, and Linda Thornburg. *Cool Careers for Girls in Computers*. Manassas Park, Va.: Impact Publications, 1999.

Rafiquzzaman, Mohamed. *Preparing for an Outstanding Career in Computers*. Diamond Bar, Calif.: Rafi Systems, 2001.

Stair, Lila B., and Leslie Stair. *Careers in Computers*. 3d ed. New York: McGraw-Hill, 2002.

Swedin, Eric G., and David L. Ferro. *Computers: The Life Story of a Technology*. Westport, Conn.: Greenwood Press, 2005.

VGM Career Books. *Resumes for Computer Careers*. 2d ed. New York: McGraw-Hill, 2002.

Wang, Wallace. *Beginning Programming for Dummies*. 4th ed. New York: For Dummies, 2006.

cation programs tell two or more computers or peripherals how to work with each other. When a system is composed of equipment from various manufacturers, networking is essential for smooth system functioning. For example, shared printers have to know how to order print jobs as they come in from various terminals. Some programmer/analysts write the code that establishes printing queues. Others might be involved in user training, since they know the software applications well. They might also customize commercial software programs to meet the needs of their company.

Many programmer/analysts become specialized in an area of business, science, or engineering. They seek education and further on-the-job training in these areas to develop expertise. They may therefore attend special seminars, workshops, and classes designed for their needs. This extra knowledge allows them to develop a deeper understanding of the computing problems specific to the business or industry.

REQUIREMENTS

High School

Take a college preparatory program with advanced classes in math, science, and computer science to prepare you for this work. This will provide a foundation of basic concepts and encourage the development of analytic and logical thinking skills. Since programmer/

analysts do a lot of proposal writing that may or may not be technical in nature, English classes are valuable as well. Speech classes will help prepare you for making formal presentations to management and clients.

Postsecondary Training

A bachelor's degree in computer science, information science, or management information systems is a minimum requirement for systems programmer/analysts. Course work in preparation for this field includes math, computer programming, science, and logic. Several years of related work experience, including knowledge of programming languages, are often necessary as well. For some very high-level positions, an advanced degree in a specific computer subfield may be required. As a result of the rapid growth of electronic commerce, some firms are also seeking analysts with a master's degree in business administration, with a concentration in information systems. Also, depending on the employer, proficiency in business, science, or engineering may be necessary.

Certification or Licensing

Some programmer/analysts pursue certification through the Institute for Certification of Computing Professionals. In particular, they take classes and exams to become certified computing professionals (CCPs). Others pursue the information systems analyst designation, which requires the completion of a four-year undergraduate information systems degree program and passing an examination. Certification is voluntary and is an added credential for job hunters. Certification demonstrates to employers that applicants have achieved a recognized level of knowledge and experience in principles and practices related to systems.

Other Requirements

Successful systems programmer/analysts demonstrate strong analytic skills and enjoy the challenges of problem solving. They are able to understand problems that exist on many levels, from technical to practical to business oriented. They can visualize complicated and abstract relationships between computer hardware and software and are good at matching needs to equipment.

Systems programmer/analysts have to be flexible as well. They routinely deal with many different kinds of people, from management to data entry clerks. Therefore, they must be knowledgeable in a lot of functional areas of the company. They should be able to talk to management about cost-effective solutions, to programmers about detailed coding, and to clerks about user-friendliness of the applications.

As is true for all computer professionals, systems programmer/analysts must be able to learn about new technology quickly. They should be naturally curious about keeping up on cutting-edge developments, which can be time consuming. Furthermore, they are often so busy at their jobs that staying in the know is done largely on their own time.

EXPLORING

You have several options to learn more about what it is like to be a computer systems programmer/analyst. You can spend a day with a working professional in this field in order to experience a typical day firsthand. Career days of this type can usually be arranged through school guidance counselors or the public relations manager of local corporations.

Strategy games, such as chess, played with friends or school clubs are a good way to put your analytic thinking skills to use while having fun. When choosing a game, the key is to make sure it relies on qualities similar to those used by programmer/analysts.

Lastly, you should become a computer hobbyist and learn everything you can about computers by working and playing with them on a daily basis. Surfing the Internet regularly, as well as reading trade magazines, will also be helpful. You might also want to try hooking up a mini-system at home or school, configuring terminals, printers, modems, and other peripherals into a coherent system. This activity requires a fair amount of knowledge and should be supervised by a professional.

EMPLOYERS

Computer systems programmer/analysts work for all types of firms and organizations that do their work on computers. Such companies may include manufacturing companies, data processing service firms, hardware and software companies, banks, insurance companies, credit companies, publishing houses, government agencies, financial institutions, Internet service providers, and colleges and universities. Many programmer/analysts are employed by businesses as consultants on a temporary or contractual basis.

STARTING OUT

Since systems programmer/analysts typically have at least some experience in a computer-related job, most are hired into these jobs from lower-level positions within the same company. For example, programmers, software engineering technicians, and network and database administrators all gain valuable computing experience that can be put to good use at a systems job. Alternatively, individuals who acquire expertise in systems programming and analysis while in other jobs may want to work with a headhunter to find the right systems positions for them. Also, trade magazines, newspapers, and employment agencies regularly feature job openings in this field.

Students in four-year degree programs should work closely with their schools' career services offices. Companies regularly work through such offices in order to find the most qualified graduates. Since it may be difficult to find a job as a programmer/analyst to begin with, it is important for students to consider their long-term potential within a certain company. The chance for promotion into a systems job can make lower-level jobs more appealing, at least in the short run.

For those individuals already employed in a computer-related job but wanting to get into systems programming and analysis, additional formal education is a good idea. Some employers have educational reimbursement policies that allow employees to take courses inexpensively. If the employee's training could directly benefit the business, companies are more willing to pay for the expense.

ADVANCEMENT

Systems programmer/analysts already occupy a relatively high-level technical job. Promotion, therefore, usually occurs in one of two directions. First, programmer/analysts can be put in charge of increasingly larger and more complex systems. Instead of concentrating on a company's local system, for example, an analyst can oversee all company systems and networks. This kind of technically based promotion can also put systems programmer/analysts into other areas of computing. With the proper experience and additional training, they can get into database or network management and design, software engineering, or even quality assurance.

The other direction in which programmer/analysts can go is management. Depending on the position sought, formal education (either a bachelor's degree in business or a master's in business administration) may be required. As more administrative duties are added, more technical ones are taken away. Therefore, programmer/analysts who enjoy the technical aspect of their work more than anything else may not want to pursue this advancement track. Excellent computing managers have both a solid background in various forms of computing and a good grasp of what it takes to run a department. Also, having the vision to see how technology will change in the short and long terms, and how those changes will affect the industry concerned, is a quality of a good manager.

EARNINGS

According to the U.S. Department of Labor, the median annual salary for computer systems analysts was $69,760 in 2006. At the low end of the pay range, 10 percent of systems analysts earned less than $42,780. The top 10 percent earned $106,820 or more. Salaries are slightly higher in geographic areas where many computer companies are clustered, such as Silicon Valley in California and Seattle, Washington.

Level of education also affects analysts' earnings. The National Association of Colleges and Employers reports that starting salaries for those with master's degrees in computer science averaged $62,727 in 2005. Those with bachelor's degrees in computer science, however, had starting salaries averaging $50,820, and those with bachelor's degrees in computer systems analysis averaged $46,189, also in 2005.

Those in senior positions can earn much higher salaries. *Computerworld* reports that senior systems analysts earned a national average of $83,390 in 2006.

Most programmer analysts receive health insurance, paid vacation, and sick leave. Some employers offer tuition reimbursement programs and in-house computer training workshops.

WORK ENVIRONMENT

Computer systems programmer/analysts work in comfortable office environments. If they work as consultants, they may travel frequently. Otherwise, travel is limited to trade shows, seminars, and visitations to vendors for demonstrations. They might also visit other businesses to observe their systems in action.

Programmer/analysts usually work 40-hour weeks and enjoy the regular holiday schedule of days off. However, as deadlines for system installation, upgrades, and spot-checking approach, they are often required to work overtime. Extra compensation for overtime hours may come in the form of time-and-a-half pay or compensatory time off, depending on the precise nature of the employee's duties, company policy, and state law. If the employer operates off-shifts, programmer/analysts may be on call to address any problems that might arise at any time of the day or night. This is relatively rare in the service sector but more common in manufacturing, heavy industry, and data processing firms.

Computer systems programming and analysis is very detailed work. The smallest error can cause major system disruptions, which can be a great source of frustration. Systems programmer/analysts must be prepared to deal with this frustration and be able to work well under pressure.

OUTLOOK

Employment for computer systems programmer/analysts will grow much faster than the average for all occupations through 2014. Increases are mainly a product of the growing number of businesses that rely extensively on computers. When businesses automate, their daily operations depend on the capacity of their computer systems to perform at desired levels. The continuous development of new technologies means that businesses must also update their old systems to remain competitive in the marketplace. Additionally, the need for businesses to network their information adds to the demand for qualified programmer/analysts. Businesses will rely increasingly on systems programmer/analysts to make the right purchasing decisions and to keep systems running smoothly.

Many computer manufacturers are beginning to expand the range of services they offer to business clients. In the years to come, they may hire many systems programmer/analysts to work as consultants on a per-project basis with a potential client. These workers would perform essentially the same duties, with the addition of extensive follow-up maintenance. They would analyze business needs and suggest proper systems to answer them. In addition, more and more independent consulting firms are hiring systems programmer/analysts to perform the same tasks.

Analysts with advanced degrees in computer science or computer engineering will be in great demand. Individuals with master's degrees in business administration with emphasis in information systems will also be highly desirable.

FOR MORE INFORMATION

For more information about systems programmer/analyst positions, contact

Association of Information Technology Professionals
401 North Michigan Avenue, Suite 2400
Chicago, IL 60611-4267
Tel: 800-224-9371
http://www.aitp.org

For information on becoming an independent consultant, contact
Independent Computer Consultants Association
11131 South Towne Square, Suite F
St. Louis, MO 63123-7817
Tel: 800-774-4222
Email: execdirector@icca.org
http://www.icca.org

For information on certification programs, contact
Institute for the Certification of Computing Professionals
2350 East Devon Avenue, Suite 115
Des Plaines, IL 60018-4610
Tel: 800-843-8227
Email: office@iccp.org
http://www.iccp.org

Credit Analysts

QUICK FACTS

School Subjects
Business
Computer science
Mathematics

Personal Skills
Communication/ideas
Leadership/management

Work Environment
Primarily indoors
Primarily one location

Minimum Education Level
Bachelor's degree

Salary Range
$30,620 to $52,350 to
$114,813+

Certification or Licensing
Voluntary

Outlook
More slowly than the average

DOT
160

GOE
13.02.04

NOC
N/A

O*NET-SOC
13-2041.00

OVERVIEW

Credit analysts analyze financial information to evaluate the amount of risk involved in lending money to businesses or individuals. They contact banks, credit associations, and others to obtain credit information and prepare a written report of findings used to recommend credit limits. There are approximately 68,000 credit analysts employed in the United States.

HISTORY

Only 50 or 75 years ago, lending money was based mainly on a person's reputation. Money was lent after a borrower talked with friends and business acquaintances. Now, of course, much more financial background information is demanded. The use of credit cards and other forms of borrowing has skyrocketed in the last several years, and today, only accepted forms of accounting are used to determine if a loan applicant is a good risk. As business and financial institutions have grown more complex, the demand for professional credit analysis has also expanded.

THE JOB

Credit analysts typically concentrate on one of two different areas. *Commercial* and *business analysts* evaluate risks in business loans; *consumer credit analysts* evaluate personal loan risks. In both cases an analyst studies financial documents such as a statement of assets and liabilities submitted by the person or company seeking the loan and consults with banks and other financial institutions that have had previous financial relationships with the applicant. Credit analysts prepare, analyze, and approve loan requests and help borrowers fill out applications.

The scope of work involved in a credit check depends in large part on the size and type of the loan requested. A background check on a $3,000 car loan, for example, is much less detailed than on a $400,000 commercial improvement loan for an expanding business. In both cases, financial statements and applicants will be checked by the credit analyst, but the larger loan will entail a much closer look at economic trends to determine if there is a market for the product being produced and the likelihood of the business failing. Because of these responsibilities, many credit analysts work solely with commercial loans.

In studying a commercial loan application, a credit analyst is interested in determining if the business or corporation is well managed and financially secure and if the existing economic climate is favorable for the operation's success. To do this, a credit analyst examines balance sheets and operating statements to determine the assets and liabilities of a company, its net sales, and its profits or losses. An analyst must be familiar with accounting and bookkeeping methods to ensure that the applicant company is operating under accepted accounting principles. A background check of the applicant company's leading officials is also done to determine if they personally have any outstanding loans. An on-site visit by the analyst may also be necessary to compare how the company's operations stack up against those of its competitors.

Analyzing economic trends to determine market conditions is another responsibility of the credit analyst. To do this, the credit analyst computes dozens of ratios to show how successful the company is in relation to similar businesses. Profit-and-loss statements, collection procedures, and a host of other factors are analyzed. This ratio analysis can also be used to measure how successful a particular industry is likely to be, given existing market considerations. Computer programs are used to highlight economic trends and interpret other important data.

The credit analyst always provides a findings report to bank executives. This report includes a complete financial history of the applicant and usually concludes with a recommendation on the loan amount, if any, that should be advanced.

REQUIREMENTS

High School

If you are interested in this career, take courses in mathematics, economics, business, and accounting in high school. You should also take English courses to develop sound oral and written language skills. Computer courses will help you to become computer literate, learn software programs, understand their applications to particular fields, and gain familiarity with accessing electronic information.

Postsecondary Training

Credit analysts usually have at least a bachelor's degree in accounting, finance, or business administration. Those who want to move up in the field often go on to obtain master's degrees in one of these subjects. Undergraduate course work should include business management, economics, statistics, and accounting. In addition, keep honing your computer skills. Some employers provide new hires with on-the-job training involving both classroom work and hands-on experience.

Certification and Licensing

The National Association of Credit Management offers the following voluntary certifications to credit professionals: credit business associate, credit business fellow, and certified credit executive. Contact the association for more information.

Other Requirements

To be a credit analyst, you should have an aptitude for mathematics and be adept at organizing, assessing, and reporting data. You must be able to analyze complex problems and devise resourceful solutions. Credit analysts also need strong interpersonal skills. You must be able to interview loan applicants and communicate effectively, establish solid working relationships with customers as well as co-workers, and clearly relate the results of your work.

EXPLORING

For the latest information on the credit management industry, check out newsgroups and Web pages on the Internet that are related to this field. For example, the National Association of Credit Management's Web site, http://www.nacm.org, has information about the field and links to other industry sites.

Consider a position as treasurer for student council or other student-run organizations. This will introduce you to the responsibilities associated with managing money. Or explore a part-time job as a bank clerk, teller, or customer service representative that will familiarize you with banking procedures. This is also a good way to network with professionals in the banking field. Various clubs and organizations may have opportunities for volunteers to develop experience working with budgets and financial statements. Join or start a business club at your school. Local institutions and small or single-owner businesses may welcome students interested in learning more about financial operations.

EMPLOYERS

Credit analysts are employed by banks, credit unions, credit agencies, business credit institutions, credit bureaus, corporations, and loan companies. They are also employed by hotels, hospitals, and department stores. Approximately 68,000 credit analysts are employed in the United States.

STARTING OUT

Although some people enter the field with a high school or two-year degree, most entry-level positions go to college graduates with degrees in fields such as accounting, finance, economics, and business administration. Credit analysts receive much of their formal training and learn specific procedures and requirements on the job. Many employees also rise through the ranks via other positions such as teller or customer service representative prior to becoming a credit analyst. Newspaper want ads, school career services offices, and direct application to specific employers are all ways of tracking down that first job.

ADVANCEMENT

Credit analysts generally advance to supervisory positions. However, promotion and salary potential are limited, and many employees often choose to leave a company for better-paying positions elsewhere. After three to five years of credit work, a skilled credit analyst can expect a promotion to *credit manager* and ultimately *chief credit executive*. Responsibilities grow to include training other credit personnel, coordinating the credit department with other internal operations, and managing relations with customers and financial institutions.

EARNINGS

Salaries of credit analysts depend on the individual's experience and education. The size of the financial institution is also a determining factor: Large banks tend to pay more than smaller operations. Salaries also increase with the number of years in the field and with a particular company. According to the U.S. Department of Labor, credit analysts had a median annual income of $52,350 in 2006. The lowest paid 10 percent earned less than $30,620, and the highest paid 10 percent earned more than $100,280. Salary.com, a Web-based recruiting firm providing salary information, reports that, in 2007, credit analysis managers had median earnings that ranged from $68,454 to $102,605, with the top 10 percent earning $114,813 or more per year. Those in senior positions often have advanced degrees.

As an added perk, many banks offer their credit analysts free checking privileges and lower interest rates on personal loans. Other benefits include health insurance, sick and vacation pay, and retirement plans.

WORK ENVIRONMENT

Most credit analysts work in typical corporate office settings that are well lighted and air conditioned in the summertime. Credit analysts can expect to work a 40-hour week, but they may have to put in overtime if a project has a tight deadline. A commercial credit analyst may have to travel to the business or corporation that is seeking a loan in order to prepare the agreement. Credit analysts can expect heavy caseloads. Respondents to the annual survey of the National Association of Credit Management reported handling 250 to 2,000 active accounts per year.

A credit analyst should be able to spend long hours behind a desk quietly reading and analyzing financial reports. Attention to detail is critical. Credit analysts can expect to work in high-pressure situations, with loans of millions of dollars dependent on their analysis.

OUTLOOK

Employment in this field is expected to grow more slowly than the average for all occupations through 2014, according to the U.S. Department of Labor. Despite this prediction, credit analysts are crucial to the success and profitability of banks and other financial organizations, and the number, variety, and complexity of credit applications are on the rise. As the field of cash management grows along with the economy and the population, banks and other financial institutions will need to hire credit analysts. Opportunities should be best for those with strong educational backgrounds and those living in urban areas that tend to have the largest and greatest number of banks and other financial institutions.

Credit analysts are particularly busy when interest rates drop and applications for loans surge. Job security is influenced by the local economy and business climate. However, loans are a major source of income for banks, and credit officers are less likely than most workers to lose their jobs in an economic downturn.

Information technology is affecting the field of credit analysis as public financial information, as well as economic and market research, becomes more accessible via the Internet. Credit professionals now have a broader range of data available upon which to base decisions.

FOR MORE INFORMATION

For general banking industry information, contact
American Bankers Association
1120 Connecticut Avenue, NW
Washington, DC 20036-3902
Tel: 800-226-5377
http://www.aba.com

For publications and information on continuing education and training programs for financial institution workers, contact
Bank Administration Institute
One North Franklin, Suite 1000
Chicago, IL 60606-3421
Tel: 888-284-4078
Email: info@bai.org
http://www.bai.org

For information on the industry, contact
Credit Research Foundation
8840 Columbia 100 Parkway
Columbia, MD 21045-2100
Tel: 410-740-5499
http://www.crfonline.org

For information on certification, continuing education, and the banking and credit industry, contact
National Association of Credit Management
8840 Columbia 100 Parkway
Columbia, MD 21045-2158
Tel: 410-740-5560
http://www.nacm.org

Demographers

QUICK FACTS

School Subjects
Computer science
Mathematics
Sociology

Personal Skills
Communication/ideas
Technical/scientific

Work Environment
Primarily indoors
One location with some
travel

Minimum Education Level
Bachelor's degree

Salary Range
$24,677 to $64,920 to
$108,630+

Certification or Licensing
None available

Outlook
More slowly than the average

DOT
054

GOE
02.04.02

NOC
2161

O*NET-SOC
15-2041.00, 19-3099.00

OVERVIEW

Demographers are population specialists who collect and analyze vital statistics related to human population changes, such as births, marriages, and deaths. They plan and conduct research surveys to study population trends and assess the effects of population movements. Demographers work for government organizations as well as at private companies across the country.

HISTORY

Population studies of one kind or another have always been of interest for various reasons. As early as the mid-1600s, for example, the English were the first to systematically record and register all births and deaths. Over the years, recording techniques were refined and expanded to conduct more sophisticated population surveys so that governments could collect information, such as number of people and extent of property holdings, to measure wealth and levy taxes.

In recent years, census taking has become much more comprehensive, and the scientific methods of collecting and interpreting demographic information have also improved extensively. Demographers now have a leading role in developing detailed population studies that are designed to reveal the essential characteristics of a society, such as the availability of health care or average income levels.

THE JOB

Demography is a social science that organizes population facts into a statistical analysis. A demographer works to establish ways in which numbers may be organized to produce new and useful information. For example, demographers may study data collected on the frequency of disease in a certain area, develop graphs and charts to plot the spread of that disease, and then forecast the probability that the medical problem may spread.

Many demographers work on the basis of a "sampling" technique in which the characteristics of the whole population are judged by taking a sample of a part of it. For example, demographers may collect data on the educational level of residents living in various locations throughout a community. They can use this information to make a projection of the average educational level of the community as a whole. In this way, demographers conduct research and forecast trends on various social and economic patterns throughout an area.

Demographers not only conduct their own surveys but also often work with statistics gathered from government sources, private surveys, and public opinion polls. They may compare different statistical information, such as an area's average income level and its population, and use it to forecast the community's future educational and medical needs. They may tabulate the average age, income, educational levels, crime rate, and poverty rate of a farming community and compare the results with the same statistics of an urban environment.

Computers have radically changed the role of the demographer. Now, much greater amounts of data can be collected and analyzed. In the Bureau of Census, for example, demographers work with material that has been compiled from the nationwide census conducted every 10 years. Millions of pieces of demographic information, such as age, gender, occupation, educational level, and country of origin, are collected from people around the country. A demographer may take this statistical information, analyze it, and then use it to forecast population growth or economic trends.

Demographers investigate and analyze a variety of social science questions for the government, such as rates of illness, availability of health and police services, and other issues that define a community. Private companies may use the information to make marketing decisions, such as where to open a new store and how best to reach possible customers.

Demographers may work on long-range planning. Population trends are especially important in such areas as educational and economic planning, and a demographer's analysis is often used to help set policy on health care issues and a host of other social concerns. Local, state, and national government agencies all use the

A demographer maps population trends. *(Bob Daemmrich, The Image Works)*

demographer's statistical forecasts in an attempt to accurately provide transportation, education, and other services.

Demographers may teach demographic research techniques to students. They also work as consultants to private businesses. Much of their time is spent doing library research, analyzing demographic information of various population groups.

An *applied statistician,* a specialized type of demographer, uses accepted theories and known statistical formulas to collect and analyze data in a specific area, such as the availability of health care in a specified location.

REQUIREMENTS

High School
Since you will need at least a bachelor's degree to find work as a demographer, you should take college preparatory courses, such as social studies, English, and mathematics (algebra and geometry) while in high school. In addition, take any statistics classes that your school offers. Training in computer science is also advantageous, as computers are used extensively for research and statistical analysis.

Postsecondary Training
College course work should include classes in social research methods, public policy, public health, statistics, and computer applica-

tions. Keep in mind that while you can get some starting jobs in the field with a bachelor's degree, most social scientists go on to attain advanced degrees. Many demographers get a doctorate in statistics, sociology, or demography. Approximately 110 universities offer master's programs in statistics, and about 60 have statistics departments offering doctorate programs.

Other Requirements
To work as a demographer, you should enjoy using logic to solve problems and have an aptitude for mathematics. You should also enjoy detailed work and must like to study and learn. Research experience is helpful. Other qualities that are helpful include intellectual curiosity and creativity, good written and oral communication skills, objectivity, and systematic work habits.

EXPLORING
A part-time or summer job at a company with a statistical research department is a good way of gaining insight into the career of demographer. Discussions with professional demographers are another way of learning about the rewards and responsibilities in this field. While in high school, ask your mathematics teach-

Books to Read

Carroll, Glenn R., and Michael T. Hannan. *The Demography of Corporations and Industries*. Princeton, N.J.: Princeton University Press, 2004.

Harrison, Paul, and Fred Pearce. *AAAS Atlas of Population and Environment*. Berkeley, Calif.: University of California Press, 2001.

Hinde, Andrew. *Demographic Methods*. London, U.K.: Arnold, 1998.

Livi-Bacci, Massimo. *A Concise History of World Population: An Introduction to Population Processes*. 4th ed. London, U.K.: Blackwell Publishing, 2006.

Preston, Samuel H., et al. *Demography: Measuring and Modeling Population Processes*. Oxford, U.K.: Blackwell Publishing, 2000.

Siegel, Jacob S., and David A. Swanson. *The Methods and Materials of Demography*. 2d ed. San Diego: Academic Press, 2004.

Weinstein, Jay A., and Vijayan K. Pillai. *Demography: The Science of Population*. Boston: Allyn & Bacon, 2000.

Yaukey, David, Douglas L. Anderton, and Jennifer Hickes Lundquist. *Demography: The Study of Human Population*. 3d ed. Prospect Heights, Ill.: Waveland Press, 2007.

ers to give you some simple statistical problems related to population changes in order to practice the kinds of statistical techniques that demographers use. Exploring statistical surveys and information from the Gallup Organization on the Internet (http://www.gallup.com) is another way to learn about this career. Additionally, undertaking your own demographic survey of an organization or group, such as your school or after-school club, is a project worth considering.

EMPLOYERS

Federal agencies such as the Census Bureau and the Bureau of Labor Statistics employ a large number of demographers, as do local and state government agencies. Private industry also may use the services of demographers, as well as universities, colleges, and foundations. Some demographers work as independent consultants rather than full-time employees for any one organization.

STARTING OUT

The usual method of entering the profession is through completion of an undergraduate or graduate degree in sociology or public health with an emphasis in demographic methods. According to Cary Davis, former vice president of the Population Reference Bureau in Washington, D.C., however, most entry-level positions require a graduate degree. "In fact," says Davis, "no one on my staff knows of any demographer who has less than a master's degree. Focus on an area that interests you, such as births and deaths or public health."

Qualified applicants can apply directly to private research firms or other companies that do population studies. University career services offices can help identify such organizations. Government jobs are listed with the Office of Personnel Management.

ADVANCEMENT

According to Cary Davis, demographers who narrow their focus and become specialized in an area of interest are most likely to advance. Those with the highest degree of education are also most likely to be promoted.

EARNINGS

Earnings vary widely according to education, training, and place of employment. Social scientists earned a median annual salary of

$64,920 in 2006, according to the U.S. Department of Labor. Those with a bachelor's degree who started work for the federal government began at $24,677 or $30,567 in 2005. Social scientists with a master's degree working for the federal government started at about $37,390, while those with a doctorate started at $45,239 or $54,221.

In 2006, statisticians (often including demographers) earned salaries that ranged from less than $37,010 to more than $108,630 annually. Those working for the federal government had mean annual salaries of $85,460. Vacation days and other benefits, such as sick leave, group insurance, and a retirement plan, are typically offered to demographers working full time for any large organization.

WORK ENVIRONMENT

Most demographers work in offices or classrooms during a regular 40-hour week. Depending on the project and deadlines, however, overtime may be required. Those engaged in research may work with other demographers assembling related information. Most of the work revolves around analyzing population data or interpreting computer information. A demographer is also usually responsible for writing a report detailing the findings. Some travel may be required, such as to attend a conference or complete limited field research.

OUTLOOK

According to the U.S. Department of Labor, careers in the social sciences are expected to grow more slowly than the average for all occupations through 2014. Those with the most training and greatest amount of education, preferably a Ph.D., should find the best job prospects. Employment opportunities should be greatest in and around large metropolitan areas, where many colleges, universities, research facilities, and federal agencies are located. Individuals with statistical training will have an advantage.

FOR MORE INFORMATION

For career publications, lists of accredited schools, and job information, contact
American Sociological Association
1307 New York Avenue, NW, Suite 700
Washington, DC 20005-4712
Tel: 202-383-9005
Email: executive.office@asanet.org
http://www.asanet.org

This organization includes demographers, sociologists, economists, public health professionals, and other individuals interested in research and education in the population field. For information on job opportunities, publications, and annual conferences and workshops, contact

Population Association of America
8630 Fenton Street, Suite 722
Silver Spring, MD 20910-3812
Tel: 301-565-6710
Email: info@popassoc.org
http://www.popassoc.org

For publications, special reports, and global population information, contact

Population Reference Bureau
1875 Connecticut Avenue, NW, Suite 520
Washington, DC 20009-5728
Tel: 800-877-9881
Email: popref@prb.org
http://www.prb.org

For population statistics, as well as information on regional offices, jobs, and a calendar of events, contact

U.S. Census Bureau
4600 Silver Hill Road
Washington, DC 20233-0001
Tel: 301-763-4748
Email: recruiter@census.gov
http://www.census.gov

Economists

OVERVIEW

Economists are concerned with how society uses resources such as land, labor, raw materials, and machinery to produce goods and services for consumption and production in the present and future. Economists study how economic systems address three basic questions: "What shall we produce?" "How shall we produce it?" and "For whom shall we produce it?" The economist then compiles, processes, and interprets the answers to these questions. There are about 13,000 economists employed in the United States.

HISTORY

Economics deals with the struggle to divide up a finite amount of goods and services to satisfy an unlimited amount of human needs and desires. No society, no matter how rich and successful, is able to produce everything needed or wanted by individuals. This reality was evident to people throughout history. In ancient Greece, the philosopher Plato discussed economic topics in his work, *The Republic,* saying the division of labor among people was the only way to supply a larger need. Individuals, he said, are not naturally self-sufficient and thus they need to cooperate in their efforts and exchange goods and services.

It was not until 1776 that the theory of economics was given a name. Adam Smith, in his work *Wealth of Nations,* described that individuals, given the opportunity to trade freely, will not create chaos. Instead, he claimed that free trade results in an orderly, logical system. His belief in this free trade system has been interpreted as an endorsement of laissez-faire capitalism, which discourages

QUICK FACTS

School Subjects
Business
Economics
Mathematics

Personal Skills
Helping/teaching
Technical/scientific

Work Environment
Primarily indoors
Primarily one location

Minimum Education Level
Master's degree

Salary Range
$24,667 to $77,010 to $136,550+

Certification or Licensing
None available

Outlook
More slowly than the average

DOT
050

GOE
02.04.02

NOC
4162

O*NET-SOC
19-3011.00, 25-1063.00

government restrictions on trade. Other economists believe that regulation is necessary to limit corruption and unfair or monopolistic practices.

The importance of economics is evidenced by its status as the only social science in which a Nobel Prize is awarded. In the last century, economics has come to be used in making a broad array of decisions within businesses, government agencies, and many other kinds of organizations.

THE JOB

Economists grapple with many issues relating to the supply and demand of goods and services and the means by which they are produced, traded, and consumed. While most economists either teach at the university level or perform research for government agencies, many work for individual for-profit or not-for-profit organizations.

Economics professors teach basic macro- and microeconomics courses as well as courses on advanced topics such as economic history and labor economics. (Macroeconomics deals with the "big picture" of economics as a whole, and microeconomics deals with individual companies and persons.) They also perform research, write papers and books, and give lectures, contributing their knowledge to the advancement of the discipline.

Government economists study national economic trends and problems; their analyses often suggest possible changes in government policy to address such issues.

For-profit and not-for-profit companies both employ economists to assess connections of organizational policy to larger business conditions and economic trends. Management often will rely on this research to make financial and other kinds of decisions that affect the company.

In their education, economists usually specialize in a particular area of interest. While the specialties of university economists range across the entire discipline, other economists' expertise generally falls into one of several categories. *Financial economists* examine the relationships among money, credit, and purchasing power to develop monetary policy and forecast financial activity. *International economists* analyze foreign trade to bring about favorable trade balances and establish trade policies. *Labor economists* attempt to forecast labor trends and recommend labor policies for businesses and government entities. *Industrial economists* study the way businesses are internally organized and suggest ways to make maximum use of assets. *Environmental economists* study the relationships between economic issues and the allocation and management of natural resources. *Agricultural economists* study food production, development in rural areas, and the allocation of natural resources.

REQUIREMENTS

High School

A strong college preparatory program is necessary in high school if you wish to enter this field. Courses in other social sciences, economics, mathematics, and English are extremely important to a would-be economist, since analyzing, interpreting, and expressing one's informed opinions about many different kinds of data are primary tasks for someone employed in this field. Also, take computer classes so that you will be able to use this research tool in college and later on. Finally, since you will be heading off to college and probably postgraduate studies, consider taking a foreign language to round out your educational background.

Postsecondary Training

A bachelor's degree with a major in economics is the minimum requirement for an entry-level position such as research assistant. A master's degree, or even a Ph.D., is more commonly required for most positions as an economist.

Typically, an economics major takes at least 10 courses on various economic topics, plus two or more mathematics courses, such as statistics and calculus or algebra. The federal government requires candidates for entry-level economist positions to have a minimum of 21 semester hours of economics and three hours of statistics, accounting, or calculus. Graduate-level courses include such specialties as advanced economic theory, econometrics, international economics, and labor economics.

Other Requirements

Economists' work is detail oriented. They do extensive research and enjoy working with abstract theories. Their research work must be precise and well documented. In addition, economists must be able to clearly explain their ideas to a range of people, including other economic experts, political leaders, and even students in a classroom.

EXPLORING

You can augment your interest in economics by taking related courses in social science and mathematics and by becoming informed about business and economic trends through reading business-related publications such as newspaper business sections and business magazines. In addition to economics course work, college students can participate in specific programs and extracurricular activities sponsored by their university's business school, such as internships with government agencies and businesses and business-related clubs and organizations.

EMPLOYERS

Approximately 13,000 economists are employed in the United States. Many economists teach at colleges and universities. Others work as researchers at government agencies, such as the U.S. Department of Labor, or international organizations, such as the United Nations. Still others find employment at not-for-profit or for-profit organizations, helping these organizations determine how to use their resources or grow in profitability. Most economics-related positions are concentrated in large cities, such as New York, Chicago, Los Angeles, and Washington, D.C., although academic positions are spread throughout the United States.

STARTING OUT

The bulletins of the various professional economic associations are good sources of job opportunities for beginning economists. Your school's career services office can also assist you in locating internships and in setting up interviews with potential employers.

ADVANCEMENT

An economist's advancement depends on his or her training, experience, personal interests, and ambition. All specialized areas provide opportunities for promotion to jobs requiring more skill and competence. Such jobs are characterized by more administrative, research, or advisory responsibilities. Consequently, promotions are governed to a great extent by job performance in the beginning fields of work. In university-level academic positions, publishing papers and books about one's research is necessary to become tenured.

EARNINGS

Economists are among the highest-paid social scientists. According to the U.S. Department of Labor, the median salary for economists was $77,010 in 2006. The lowest paid 10 percent made less than $42,280, and the highest paid 10 percent earned more than $136,550.

The U.S. Department of Labor reports that economists employed by the federal government earned mean annual salaries of $94,400 in 2006. Starting salaries for federal government economists vary by degree attained. Economists with a bachelor's degree earned approximately $24,667 or $30,567 in 2005, depending on their academic record; economists with a master's degree earned approximately $37,390; and those with a Ph.D., $45,239 or $54,221 depending on their level of experience. College economics educators earned salaries that ranged from less than $38,630 to $130,990 or more in 2006, according to the U.S. Department of Labor. Educators employed at colleges and universities had mean annual earnings of $83,420, while those employed at junior colleges earned $61,150 a year.

Private-industry economists' salaries can be much higher, into the six figures. Notably, in a study published in *Money* magazine, economists' salaries tended to be 3.1 times higher at mid-career than their starting salaries. According to the survey, this is a higher increase than in any other profession; lawyers made 2.77 times more and accountants 2.21 times more in their mid-careers than at the start. Benefits such as vacation and insurance are comparable to those of workers in other organizations.

WORK ENVIRONMENT

Economists generally work in offices or classrooms. The average workweek is 40 hours, although academic and business economists' schedules often can be less predictable. Economists in nonteaching positions often work alone writing reports, preparing statistical charts, and using computers, but they may also be part of a research team. Most economists work under deadline pressure and sometimes must work overtime. Regular travel may be necessary to collect data or to attend conferences or meetings.

OUTLOOK

The employment of economists is expected to grow more slowly than average for all occupations through 2014, according to the U.S. Department of Labor. Most openings will occur as economists retire, transfer to other job fields, or leave the profession for other reasons. Economists employed by private industry—especially in management, scientific, and technical consulting services—will enjoy the best prospects. In the academic arena, economists with master's and doctoral degrees will face strong competition for desirable teaching jobs. The demand for secondary school economics teachers is expected to grow. Economics majors with only bachelor's degrees will experience the greatest employment difficulty, although their analytical skills can lead to positions in related fields such as management and sales. Those who meet state certification requirements may wish to become secondary school economics teachers, as demand for teachers in this specialty is expected to increase.

FOR MORE INFORMATION

For information on agricultural economics and a list of colleges that offer programs in the field, contact
American Agricultural Economics Association
555 East Wells Street, Suite 1100
Milwaukee, WI 53202-3800
Tel: 414-918-3190
Email: info@aaea.org
http://www.aaea.org

For information on job listings and resources of interest to economists, contact
American Economic Association
2014 Broadway, Suite 305
Nashville, TN 37203-2425
Tel: 615-322-2595
Email: info@econlit.org
http://www.aeaweb.org

For information on graduate programs in environmental and resource economics, contact
Association of Environmental and Resource Economists
1616 P Street, NW, Suite 600
Washington, DC 20036-1434
Tel: 202-328-5125
http://www.aere.org

To read the publication Careers in Business Economics, *check out the following Web site:*
National Association for Business Economics
1233 20th Street, NW, Suite 505
Washington, DC 20036-2365

Tel: 202-463-6223
Email: nabe@nabe.com
http://www.nabe.com

The NCEE promotes the economic education of students from kindergarten through 12th grade. It offers teacher training courses and materials. For more information, contact
National Council on Economic Education (NCEE)
1140 Avenue of the Americas
New York, NY 10036-5803
Tel: 800-338-1192
http://www.ncee.net

For information on membership and job listings, contact
Society of Government Economists
PO Box 77082
Washington, DC 20013-8082
http://www.sge-econ.org

Engineers

QUICK FACTS

School Subjects
Mathematics
Physics

Personal Skills
Leadership/management
Technical/scientific

Work Environment
Indoors and outdoors
Primarily multiple locations

Minimum Education Level
Bachelor's degree

Salary Range
$41,050 to $67,810 to
$135,260+

Certification or Licensing
Voluntary (certification)
Required for certain positions
(licensing)

Outlook
About as fast as the average

DOT
003, 005, 007, 008, 010,
012, 013, 014, 015, 019,
024, 638, 950, 953

GOE
02.07.01, 02.07.02, 02.07.03,
02.07.04

NOC
2122, 2131, 2132, 2133,
2134, 2141, 2142, 2143,
2144, 2145, 2147, 2148,
2173, 4121

O*NET-SOC
17-2000s: 17-2011.00 to
17-2199.99

OVERVIEW

Engineers are problem-solvers who use the principles of mathematics and science to plan, design, and create ways to make things work better. Engineers are needed in every field imaginable, from agricultural engineering, where they work to improve farming methods and increase food production, to civil engineering where they design bridges, highways, dams, and other large projects. Engineers work in fields involving electricity, pollution control, automotives, water resources, space exploration, and many, many others. In fact, more than 25 engineering specialties are recognized by professional engineering societies. There are approximately 1.4 million engineers employed in the United States.

HISTORY

Building has been one of humanity's basic activities. The development of civilization is marked by the building of pyramids, bridges, roadways, temples, aqueducts, walls and fortifications, canals, and many other structures. These projects were designed and supervised by the earliest form of civil engineers. These engineers had to design methods of moving large and cumbersome stones for buildings, sometimes across a long distance. To accomplish this without the benefit of motorized vehicles, early engineers designed rollers, pulleys, levers, and hydraulics. The understanding of force and counterforce allowed the engineers to design

At a research station, an agricultural engineer (right) and mechanical engineer perform quarterly service on a wind turbine. *(Stephen Ausmus, Agricultural Research Service, U.S. Department of Agriculture)*

ways to decrease the physical effort needed by the builders to move massive stones. Without this, structures like the pyramids would not have been possible.

Chemical engineering methods were applied early on to create fermented drinks, such as beer and wine. Separating curds from whey to create cheese also required engineering principles. When developing fuel for heat and lighting, amateur chemical engineers created oils from animal blubber. The first petroleum engineers separated kerosene from petroleum; then gasoline, a by-product of kerosene production, was recognized as a good fuel product at the end of the 1800s.

Aeronautical engineering, one of the most fascinating engineering fields, had the longest period of time without a single success. Leonardo da Vinci is one of the many who tried to design machines that would allow people to fly; it wasn't until 1783 that the first person "flew." Joseph Michel and Jacques Etienne Montgolfier launched the first successful hot air balloon. It took another 110 years for aeronautical engineers to find another method of flying besides the balloon. Otto Lilienthal developed a glider airplane. And the famous Wright brothers, Orville and Wilbur, successfully flew a motorized airplane for the first time in 1903.

Many of the engineering fields are products of the 20th century. Nuclear, biotechnical, petroleum, computer, and electronic engineering fields all developed during this century. Cars, airplanes, computers, televisions, telephones, and even movies are all engineering developments of the past century. Engineers have influenced discoveries and inventions more than workers in any other profession. The work of engineers has a more thorough impact on all human life than any other discipline.

THE JOB

Engineers, whatever scientific field they are in, engage in one of five areas of study: The first stage of any project is research. Engineers who work in research are responsible for investigating new materials, processes, or principles for practical applications of ideas and materials. For example, a *research engineer* might research the properties and principals of radar.

Development follows research. Engineers working in the area of development take the results of the research and begin thinking about how best to apply them to their practical functions. A *development engineer* might develop a plan for using properties of radar in tracking weather systems.

Application is the actual production of an idea developed. Engineers take the product from development and establish ways of designing and producing the materials, machines, methods, or other results of research and development. It is at this stage that the concepts become usable to the people outside of engineering. Taking the radar example, a new radar device for tracking and monitoring hurricanes may be created in applied engineering. It isn't until this stage that the research and development areas affect the average person. However, the applications area would not exist if it weren't for the other two.

Management and maintenance are the final stages of engineering work. These engineers are responsible for keeping the developed idea working. Without some form of upkeep and improvement, engineering discoveries would be lost.

Engineers are intricately involved in the development of almost all new products. They must design and test all new components and fit them together into an overall plan. Engineers also make sure the product can be manufactured safely and economically. The product may be as simple as a child's toy or as complex as a missile launcher or spacecraft.

Because the work they perform is so specific to one branch of science, there are engineers for every scientific discipline. The following paragraphs briefly describe engineering specialties. It is important to remember that experts in each branch of engineering have knowledge that can be used in many of the fields. Mechanical engineers, for example, might work in aerospace engineering, automotives, medicine, or oceanography.

Aerospace and aeronautical engineers are involved in the development, design, and assembly of all types of aircraft. Such structures include missiles, spacecraft, airplanes, engines, and other related equipment.

Agricultural engineers are concerned with improving farming methods and increasing food production. They design farm equipment, develop irrigation systems, coordinate food-processing systems, and install land reclamation projects.

Automotive engineers are employed by car and truck manufacturers and component suppliers to design and build vehicles. They may work with engine design, aerodynamics, fuel efficiency, safety features, and more.

Biomedical engineers are highly trained scientists who apply engineering and life science principles to problems in medical research and health care. They design health care instruments and devices or apply engineering principles to the study of human systems.

Chemical engineers develop, research, and produce a variety of substances for commercial sale such as detergents, plastics, and medicine. They are interested in taking scientific knowledge from the field of chemistry and applying it to human use. Chemical engineers might work to create cleaner fuels for automobiles or develop more effective and environmentally safer fertilizers.

Civil engineers design and supervise the construction of bridges, highways, dams, waste management systems, and other large projects. Civil engineers also work for governments in city planning and are needed whenever any type of large construction or renovation occurs.

Transportation engineers are civil engineering specialists who plan, design, and operate all methods, structures, and systems that transport people and goods in a safe, convenient, rapid, and environmentally responsible manner. Typical projects they work on are streets, highways, tollways, airports, transit systems, railroads, and harbors.

Electrical engineers concentrate on the generation, transmission, and distribution of electricity. In addition, they develop and improve electrical equipment and appliances. They also may consult in the planning of electric power plants. Electrical engineers are needed in any field that involves electricity, which means that they are widely employed and their jobs vary greatly. *Electronics engineers* are electrical engineers who specialize in electronics equipment. They design, develop, and test products such as computers, electronics, medical devices, and communications equipment.

Fire protection engineers develop ways to prevent fires in all types of structures. They often work as consultants during the construction of buildings and industrial plants, designing fire prevention methods. In addition to prevention, they also devise plans for disposing of post-fire refuse, particularly those from chemical fires.

Computer *hardware engineers* design, build, and test computer hardware (such as computer chips and circuit boards) and computer systems. They also work with peripheral devices such as printers, scanners, modems, and monitors, among others. Hardware engineers are employed by a variety of companies, some of which specialize in business, accounting, science, or engineering.

Industrial engineers are responsible for the layout, design, equipment, and systems of large plants, campuses, medical centers, and other large, sprawling complexes. They work with architects and contractors to ensure safe, productive, and comfortable facilities on a large scale. They are involved in quality and production control, cost analysis, sales engineering, and other industrial concerns. Two subsections of this field are *facilities engineering* and *manufacturing engineering*.

Marine engineers are involved in the construction of maritime vessels. They work with naval architects to design the most efficient and cost-effective ships. They also are called on by energy companies involved in underwater exploration.

Materials engineers develop and test materials for specific products. They study plans for new products and recommend the appropriate materials to be used, such as metals, alloys, composites, ceramics, polymers, fibers, or other appropriate substances. *Ceramic engineers* are materials engineers who work with nonmetallic minerals, clay, and silicates to create ceramic products. Such products range from light bulbs to exterior tiles on spacecraft. Ceramic engineers study the properties of the materials they use and design heat-resistant products such as porcelain, glass, bricks, and coatings for industrial equipment. Ceramics is an expanding field of study. *Metallurgical engineers* are specialized materials engineers who work with metals. Typically, their jobs fall into two categories: extractive metallurgists and physical metallurgists. *Extractive metallurgists* are involved with the removal of ore, the separation of metal from the ore, and the processing of the extracted metals. *Physical metallurgists* study metals and related alloys, finding more efficient means of converting them into final products. *Plastics engineers* are specialized materials engineers who create, design, and test polymeric materials to manufacture useful end products, from plastic automobile parts, to biodegradable polymers for a packaging company, to plastic fibers for clothing.

In general, *mechanical engineers* design motors and machines that generate power. Such products include automobiles and their engines, refrigerators, machine tools, presses, and nuclear reactors. Due to the all-encompassing nature of their tasks, mechanical engineers are involved in nearly all types of industry.

Mining engineers work on mining projects ranging from surveying the land to designing shafts. They study the cost-effectiveness of mining projects and design means of transporting the mined ore to the surface.

Nuclear engineers develop products that either create or use nuclear energy. They design and monitor the operation of nuclear power plants, ensuring their efficiency and safety. In addition, they develop new uses for nuclear technology in industry and in medicine.

Optical engineers design equipment for such instruments as cameras and telescopes. They work on all forms of equipment that enhance visual ability or reception. For example, an optical engineer might help develop miniature cameras for satellites in space exploration.

Packaging engineers design the packaging for consumer goods such as food, electronics, medical products, toys, appliances, clothing, and other items. Packages are designed to protect products, provide benefit to consumers, conserve natural resources, and minimize waste through recycling.

After an oil or gas field has been discovered, it is up to *petroleum engineers* to choose a drilling method and supervise the drilling operation. Petroleum engineers are always looking for ways to recover oil reserves from remote locations and to increase oil output.

Pollution control engineers design systems that curb pollution. These systems include solid waste management, noise abatement, water quality control, and air filtering. Pollution control engineers who work for the government set standards for allowable pollutants in the environment.

Project engineers are in charge of entire engineering projects. They are responsible for scheduling and overseeing every stage of a project, ensuring that each stage is completed in an efficient and timely fashion. They must make sure that the project is completed according to standard procedures and regulations.

Quality control engineers plan and direct procedures and activities involved in the processing and production of materials and goods in order to ensure specified standards of quality. They select the best techniques for a specific process or method, determine the level of quality needed, and take the necessary action to maintain or improve quality performance.

Robotics engineers design, develop, build, and program robots and robotic devices, including peripheral equipment and computer software used to control robots. The title robotics engineer may be used to refer to any engineer who works primarily with robots. In many cases, these engineers may have been trained as mechanical, electronic, computer, or manufacturing engineers. A small, but growing, number of engineers trained specially in robotics are graduating from colleges and universities with robotics engineering or closely related degrees.

Safety engineers are concerned with preventing accidents. They work in many different branches of engineering, from mechanical to transportation engineering. Safety engineers may study ergonomics to develop human-friendly machines that reduce repetitive motion disorders, or they may plan fire evacuation plans for a large factory or office complex. Safety engineers work at construction sites, environmental hazard spots, insurance companies, transportation offices, and similar workplaces.

Computer *software engineers* are responsible for customizing existing software programs to meet the needs and desires of a particular business or industry. First, they spend considerable time researching, defining, and analyzing the problem at hand. Then,

Median Annual Earnings for Engineers, 2006

Aerospace engineers	$87,610
Agricultural engineers	$66,030
Biomedical engineers	$73,930
Chemical engineers	$78,860
Civil engineers	$68,600
Electrical engineers	$75,930
Electronics engineers	$81,050
Environmental engineers	$69,940
Hardware engineers	$88,470
Industrial engineers	$68,620
Marine engineers	$72,990
Materials engineers	$73,990
Mechanical engineers	$69,850
Mining/Geological engineers	$72,160
Nuclear engineers	$90,220
Petroleum engineers	$98,380
Safety engineers	$66,290

Source: U.S. Department of Labor

they develop software programs to resolve the problem on the computer.

Soils engineers study the grounds on which proposed buildings will be constructed to determine whether the ground is suitable for construction. Soils engineers must take into account any environmental problems that may occur such as strong winds, earthquakes, or heavy rains.

Engineers are assisted by *engineering technicians and technologists*. These workers are employed in all engineering disciplines, and are differentiated most commonly by the type of education they receive. Engineering technicians typically have an associate degree in engineering technology, although some learn their skills via a combination of postsecondary training and on-the-job training. Engineering technologists typically have a bachelor's degree in engineering technology. Some engineering technicians and technologists pursue advanced education and become engineers.

REQUIREMENTS

High School

High school students interested in engineering should take a great deal of mathematics, including geometry, trigonometry, calculus, and two years of algebra. They should develop a strong background in physics, chemistry, biology, and computer programming or applications. Because engineers must communicate constantly with other engineers, scientists, clients, and consumers, four years of language arts are essential.

Postsecondary Training

After high school, students should proceed to a four-year college or university to earn a bachelor's degree in engineering. Some engineers major in a science such as physics, computers, or chemistry and then find work applying their science in an engineering field or go to graduate school for a master's or doctorate degree in engineering. Many engineers, no matter their undergraduate major, now pursue advanced degrees in the field.

Certification and Licensing

Many engineers become certified. Certification is a status granted by a technical or professional organization for the purpose of recognizing and documenting an individual's abilities in a specific engineering field.

Licensure as a professional engineer is recommended since an increasing number of employers require it. Even those employers who do not require licensing will view it favorably when considering new hires or when reviewing workers for promotion. Licensing requirements vary from state to state. In general, however, they involve having graduated from an accredited school, having four years of work experience, and having passed the eight-hour Fundamentals of Engineering exam and the eight-hour Principles and Practice of Engineering exam. Depending on your state, you can take the Fundamentals exam shortly before your graduation from college or after you have received your bachelor's degree. At that point you will be an engineer-in-training (EIT). Once you have fulfilled all the licensure requirements, you receive the designation professional engineer (PE). Visit the National Council of Examiners for Engineering and Surveying's Web site, http://www.ncees.org, for more information on licensure.

Other Requirements

Students who are interested in becoming engineers should enjoy solving problems, developing logical plans, and designing things.

They should have a strong interest and ability in science and mathematics. Engineers often work on projects in teams, so prospective engineers should be able to work well both alone and with others.

EXPLORING

Perhaps the best way to explore the field of engineering is by contacting the Junior Engineering Technical Society (JETS). JETS can help you learn about different fields within engineering and can guide you toward science and engineering fairs.

Participation in science and engineering fairs can be an invaluable experience for high school students interested in engineering. Through these fairs, you will learn to do your own research and applications in an engineering field. Too often, students leave high school with a strong academic background in mathematics and sciences, but have never applied their knowledge to the real world. By developing a project for a fair, you can begin to learn how to think like an engineer by creatively using your academic knowledge to solve real-life problems.

EMPLOYERS

Approximately 1.4 million engineers are employed in the United States—with many millions more employed throughout the world. Since engineering is such a broad field, there are literally thousands of different places where engineers can find employment, depending on their specialty. Engineers are needed in virtually every field. For example, mechanical, automobile, chemical, industrial, plastics, and robotics engineers may find employment with one of the major U.S. automobile makers, as well as any of the thousands of private manufacturing companies. Aeronautical or aerospace engineers will almost certainly try to land a job at NASA or a major commercial firm like Boeing. Civil engineers can find jobs with local and city governments, with construction firms, with the military or federal government, and even large corporations. The petroleum and chemical engineer can seek jobs, naturally, with petroleum and gas companies like BP, Texaco, and Exxon, or they can look for jobs with major chemical companies like Dow Chemical, Eastman Chemical Company, or DuPont. Environmental and biological engineers will have no problem finding employers at the Environmental Protection Agency, industry, or consulting firms. Companies producing high-tech equipment for commercial and industrial use look for skilled electrical engineers, as well as software, mechanical, materials, and plastics engineers.

Engineers are also employed by local, state, and the federal government—194,000 in 2004, according to the U.S. Department of Labor. Some federal employers of engineers include the National Aeronautics and Space Administration, and the Departments of Agriculture, Defense, Energy, Homeland Security, Interior, and Transportation.

Other possibilities for engineers can be found in academia as instructors or researchers or as writers for engineering-oriented publications.

STARTING OUT

College and graduate school programs can help newly degreed engineers locate jobs. These schools are often in touch with prospective employers who are in need of engineers. Conferences, trade shows, and engineering career fairs can also be good places for new engineers to begin meeting employers and setting up interviews. The American Association of Engineering Societies maintains a membership list of the various engineering societies of each field, such as agriculture or mining. College graduates can contact these societies to find out about gaining employment in the field, calendars of events such as conferences or fairs, and more.

ADVANCEMENT

As engineers gain more experience they are given greater responsibilities and tougher problems to solve. At this stage, the engineer will be involved in more decision making and independent work. Some engineers advance to become engineering team managers or supervisors of entire projects. They also may enter administrative or sales positions. In addition, many high level corporate and government executives started out as engineers.

Advancement depends upon experience and education. The more experience engineers get, the more independence and responsibilities they will probably gain; however, an engineer with a bachelor's degree will, in all probability, not make it to the highest levels of the field. Engineers who are interested in going into corporate, industrial, or executive positions often go back to school to earn degrees in law or business.

EARNINGS

Engineers earn some of the highest starting salaries of any career. In 2005, engineers with a bachelor's degree earned salaries that ranged from $43,679 (civil engineers) to $61,516 (petroleum engineers), according to the National Association of Colleges and Employers. Engineers with a master's degree earned starting salaries that ranged from $48,050 (civil engineers) to $64,416 (electrical/electronics engineers). Overall, in 2006 average salaries for engineers ranged from less than $41,050 (safety engineers) to $135,260 (computer hardware engineers) or more annually, according to the U.S. Department of Labor.

Engineers who work for a company usually receive benefits such as vacation days, sick leave, health and life insurance, and a savings and pension program. Self-employed engineers must provide their own benefits.

WORK ENVIRONMENT

Engineers usually have a central office from which they base their work, and these offices are typically quite pleasant, clean, and climate-controlled. Engineers often have clerical, research, and technical staffs working for them at these offices.

Most engineers, however, are required to spend at least part of their time on a specific work site, and these sites may be noisy, dusty, dirty, and unpleasant. Engineers may find themselves at construction sites and "hard hat" areas, on assembly lines and runways, at sewage treatment plants, in underground culverts and pipelines, and at machine shops, dairy farms, and drill rigs. People interested in becoming engineers should be flexible about work sites and adjust easily to different types of environments.

While it is fun to solve problems and develop innovations, engineering is a serious job. People rely on engineers in some way for their safety and well-being. They want to be sure that their houses and offices are sturdy, their cars safe, and their food is processed and packaged safely. Because technology has become so omnipresent in society, people have become accustomed to trusting engineers with their safety. A good engineer must work to be deserving of this trust.

OUTLOOK

Employment for engineers is expected to grow about as fast as the average for all occupations through 2014, according to the U.S. Department of Labor. A large number of engineers have traditionally been employed in manufacturing, but while engineers in these industries will continue to be needed, not much employment growth is expected due to technological advancements and the trend by manufacturing companies to relocate their plants to foreign countries. Overall, environmental and biomedical engineers will enjoy the strongest demand. The war on terrorism has also created growth in defense- and homeland security-related engineering industries.

Engineers have traditionally enjoyed great employment security because their work is so essential to maintaining and advancing America's infrastructure and industry. Even in times of economic decline, engineers' jobs are generally safe. Engineers who stay current concerning the latest technologies and remain flexible in regards to type of employer, location, and other factors will most likely ensure themselves of employment for years to come.

FOR MORE INFORMATION

For a list of accredited schools and colleges, contact
Accreditation Board for Engineering and Technology Inc.
111 Market Place, Suite 1050
Baltimore, MD 21202-7116
Tel: 410-347-7700
http://www.abet.org

For information on engineering associations, contact
American Association of Engineering Societies
1620 I Street, NW, Suite 210
Washington, DC 20006-4028
Tel: 202-296-2237
http://www.aaes.org

For information on careers in engineering, contact
American Society for Engineering Education
1818 N Street, NW, Suite 600
Washington, DC 20036-2479
Tel: 202-331-3500
http://www.asee.org

For information on engineering careers and students clubs and competitions, contact
Junior Engineering Technical Society
1420 King Street, Suite 405
Alexandria, VA 22314-2794
Tel: 703-548-5387
Email: info@jets.org
http://www.jets.org

For information on licensure, contact
National Council of Examiners for Engineering and Surveying
PO Box 1686
Clemson, SC 29633-1686
Tel: 800-250-3196
http://www.ncees.org

For information on licensure and practice areas, contact
National Society of Professional Engineers
1420 King Street
Alexandria, VA 22314-2794
Tel: 703-684-2800
http://www.nspe.org

The following Web site offers a variety of useful resources to inspire young women to pursue careers in engineering
Engineer Girl!
http://www.engineergirl.org

INTERVIEW

Jackie Schirmer is a mechanical engineer for Washington Group International in Denver, Colorado. She discussed her career with the editors of Careers in Focus: Mathematics and Physics.

Q. How long have you been a mechanical engineer?
A. I have been a mechanical engineer for almost 10 years. I began working at my current employer, Washington Group International, right out of college. Although I thought I would leave after about two years, I found the work was exciting, diverse, and challenging—so I have stayed!

Q. Why did you decide to become a mechanical engineer?
A. Ever since I was a little girl, I was excited about the space program, airplanes, my dad's radio equipment, chemistry experiments in the kitchen, and building forts and dams in my backyard. Then, when I was in middle school, a friend of mine was severely hurt in an accident where they were unable to help him walk again because the technology wasn't available yet. This was very disturbing to me, and I decided that mechanical engineering was a field where I could help further technological advances to help people like my friend as well as work in an area where I had a natural passion for technology, design, and invention.

Q. What do you like most and least about your career?

A. As a mechanical engineer at Washington Group, I have the opportunity to make a positive impact on the world through not only my strengths and knowledge, but also by leveraging the brainpower and visions of the people I work with. I love the challenge and excitement of this, and it keeps me coming back whether I am building rocket launch facilities, chemical weapons disposal plants, or schools in Iraq. Being able to make this difference is what I like the most. However, sometimes my passion for my work and needs of the job can be too overbearing, and it is a constant juggle to keep balance in my life and make time for my family and friends. It's not that I don't enjoy the people I work with, but the time away from those I love is what I like least—pretty much a given with any job!

Q. What are the three most important professional qualities for mechanical engineers?

A. First, mechanical engineers must have integrity and candor. People's lives can be on the line if you are not straightforward with the limitations or intent of the items you are creating. Second, mechanical engineers must be willing to work with others. Mechanical engineers often interface and coordinate with structural, instrument and control, electrical, chemical, or other engineers, and may also interface with the end-user of the design or product. Third, it is critical that mechanical engineers be willing to learn and think out of the box. The answers will not always be right in front of you—that is what you are there for!

Q. What advice would you give to high school students who are interested in this career?

A. Obviously, take as many math, science, and computer classes as you can so you can be accepted into an engineering degree program. What is not obvious is that the pace is a lot slower in high school and gives you a good chance to establish a base for more in-depth learning in college. If nothing else, you will have more time for a social life in college if you get ahead early.

Internships or summer jobs with a technical company are also good steps toward understanding company culture, industry trends, and types of opportunities to target your college degree toward. This is true even with the "menial" jobs they often give to students.

Some schools offer science, technology, or computer clubs—all of which are a good idea to give you a step up. I was in Civil

Air Patrol, which gave me multiple opportunities to gain insight and make contacts in the aerospace field. These types of activities can help you hone in to find your primary areas of interest, but I also believe it is important to be involved in community organizations and/or sports in order to balance your understanding of the world.

Stick with it. It is hard, but the payoffs are unbeatable. An engineering degree opens any door you choose.

Q. What is the future employment outlook in the field?

A. The future employment outlook is wide open and very bright for mechanical engineers. The world is changing faster and faster every day, and engineers are right in front of the pack leading this change. You can't go wrong with a career or even a base degree in this field.

Financial Planners

QUICK FACTS

School Subjects
Business
Mathematics

Personal Skills
Helping/teaching
Leadership/management

Work Environment
Primarily indoors
Primarily one location

Minimum Education Level
Bachelor's degree

Salary Range
$32,340 to $66,120 to
$283,000+

Certification or Licensing
Recommended (certification)
Required for certain positions (licensing)

Outlook
Faster than the average

DOT
250

GOE
12.03.01

NOC
1114

O*NET-SOC
13-2052.00, 41-3031.01,
41-3031.02

OVERVIEW

Financial planning is the process of establishing financial goals and creating ways to reach them. Certified *financial planners* examine the assets of their clients and suggest what steps they need to take in the future to meet their goals. They take a broad approach to financial advice, which distinguishes them from other professional advisers, such as insurance agents, stockbrokers, accountants, attorneys, and real estate agents, each of whom typically focuses on only one aspect of a person's finances.

HISTORY

Except for the depression years of the 1930s and intermittent recessions, the United States economy expanded impressively after World War I. As the average American's income increased, so did lifestyle expectations. By the 21st century, vacations to Disney World, cell phones for everyone in the family, two or three cars in the garage, and thoughts of a financially worry-free retirement were not uncommon. But how do Americans meet such high expectations? More and more have begun turning to professionals—financial planners—who recommend financial strategies. According to a consumer survey done by the Certified Financial Planner Board of Standards (CFP Board), 42 percent of respondents said they had experience with financial planners. In addition, 25 percent were currently using the services of a financial planner. Fee-only planners were the most popular, with 47 percent of respondents noting that they preferred to work with a financial planner who is compensated this way instead of by commission or other means. Fee-only financial planners represent a growing segment of the financial advising industry, but the profession as a whole is booming due to the deregulation of certain institutions dealing with money. Because of this deregulation, banks, brokerage firms, and insurance companies have been allowed to offer more financial services—including investment advice—to customers since 1999. This has created many job openings for planners who want to work for these businesses.

Other reasons for growth in this industry include the large number of people (baby boomers, born between 1946 and 1964) who are closing in on or reaching retirement age and taking stock of their assets. As boomers consider if they have enough money to pay for the retirement they want, more and more of them are turning to financial planners for advice about such things as annuities, long-term health insurance, and individual retirement accounts. Another factor that has spurred growth is the increased awareness people have about investing and other options because of the large amount of financial information now directed at the general public. Today commercials for brokerage firms, television talk shows with weekly money advice, and financial publications and Web sites all offer various news and tips about what the average person should do with his or her money. All this information can be overwhelming, and people turn to experts for help. According to the CFP Board's survey, 70 percent of respondents felt that financial advisers were a good source of information about financial products. As tax laws change, the world economy becomes more complex, and new technologies alter workforces, financial planners will continue to be in demand for their expert advice.

THE JOB

Financial planners advise their clients on many aspects of finance. Although they seem to be jacks-of-all-trades, certified financial planners do not work alone; they meet with their clients' other advisers, such as attorneys, accountants, trust officers, and investment bankers. Financial planners fully research their clients' overall financial picture. After meeting with the clients and their other advisers, certified financial planners analyze the data they have received and generate a written report that includes their recommendations on how the clients can best achieve their goals. This report details the clients' financial objectives, current income, investments, risk tolerance, expenses, tax returns, insurance coverage, retirement programs, estate plans, and other important information.

Financial planning is an ongoing process. The plan must be monitored and reviewed periodically so that adjustments can be made, if necessary, to assure that it continues to meet individual needs.

The plan itself is a set of recommendations and strategies for clients to use or ignore, and financial planners should be ready to answer hard questions about the integrity of the plans they map out. After all, they are dealing with all of the money and investments that people have worked a lifetime accruing.

People need financial planners for different things. Some might want life insurance, college savings plans, or estate planning. Sometimes these needs are triggered by changes in people's lives, such as retirement, death of a spouse, disability, marriage, birth of children, or job changes. Certified financial planners spend the majority of their time on the following topics: investment planning, retirement planning, tax planning, estate planning, and risk management. All of these areas require different types of financial knowledge, and planners are generally expected to be extremely competent in the disciplines of asset management, employee benefits, estate planning, insurance, investments, and retirement, according to the Certified Financial Planner Board of Standards. A financial planner must also have good interpersonal skills, since establishing solid client-planner relationships is essential to the planner's success. It also helps to have good communication skills, since even the best financial plan, if presented poorly to a client, can be rejected.

Clients drive the job of financial planners. The advice planners provide depends on their clients' particular needs, resources, and priorities. Many people think they cannot afford or do not need a comprehensive financial plan. Certified financial planners must have a certain amount of expertise in sales to build their client base.

Certified financial planners use various ways to develop their client lists, including telephone solicitation, giving seminars on financial planning to the general public or specific organizations, and networking with social contacts. Referrals from satisfied customers also help the business grow.

Although certified financial planners are trained in comprehensive financial planning, some specialize in one area, such as asset management, investments, or retirement planning. In most small or self-owned financial planning companies, they are generalists. However, in some large companies, planners might specialize in particular areas, including insurance, real estate, mutual funds, annuities, pensions, or business valuations.

REQUIREMENTS

High School

If financial planning sounds interesting to you, take as many business classes as possible as well as mathematics. Communication courses, such as speech or drama, will help put you at ease when talking in front of a crowd, something financial planners must do occasionally. English courses will help you prepare the written reports planners present to their clients.

Postsecondary Training

Earning a bachelor's degree starts financial planners on the right track, but it will help if your degree indicates a skill with numbers, be it in science or business. A business administration degree with a specialization in financial planning or a liberal arts degree with courses in accounting, business administration, economics, finance, marketing, human behavior, counseling, and public speaking is excellent preparation for this sort of job.

Certification or Licensing

However, education alone will not motivate clients to turn over their finances to you. Many financial professionals are licensed on the state and federal levels in financial planning specialties, such as stocks and insurance. The Securities and Exchange Commission and most states have licensing requirements for investment advisers, a category under which most financial planners also fall. However, the government does not regulate most of the activities of planners. Therefore, to show credibility to clients, most financial planners choose to become certified as either a certified financial planner (CFP) or a chartered financial consultant (ChFC).

To receive the CFP mark of certification, offered by the CFP Board, candidates must meet what the board refers to as the four E's, which comprise the following:

Education: To be eligible to take the certification exam, candidates must meet education requirements in one of the following ways. The first option is to complete a CFP board-registered program in financial planning. The second is to hold a specific degree and professional credentials in one of several areas the board has approved of; these include certified public accountant, licensed attorney, chartered financial consultant, chartered life underwriter, chartered financial analyst, doctor of business administration, and Ph.D. in business or economics. The final option is for applicants to submit transcripts of their undergraduate or graduate education to the board for review. If the board feels the education requirements have been met, the candidate may sit for the exam. Additionally, applicants must have a bachelor's degree in any area of study or program to obtain CFP certification. They do not need to have earned this degree at the time they take the examination, but must show proof of completion of this degree in order to complete the final stage of certification.

Examination: Once candidates have completed the education requirements, they may take the certification exam, which tests knowledge on various key aspects of financial planning.

Experience: Either before or after passing the certification exam, candidates must have three years of work experience.

Ethics: After candidates have completed the education, examination, and experience requirements, they must voluntarily ascribe to the CFP Board's Code of Ethics and Professional Responsibility and Financial Planning Practice Standards to be allowed to use the CFP mark. This voluntary agreement empowers the board to take action if a CFP licensee violates the code. Such violations could lead to disciplinary action, including permanent revocation of the right to use the CFP mark.

The American College offers the ChFC designation. To receive this designation, candidates must complete certain course work stipulated by The American College, meet experience requirements, and agree to uphold The American College's Code of Ethics and Procedures.

To maintain the CFP and the ChFC designations, professionals will need to meet continuing education and other requirements as determined by the CFP Board and The American College.

OTHER REQUIREMENTS

Other factors that contribute to success as a financial planner include keeping up with continuing education, referrals from clients, specialization, people and communication skills, and a strong educational background.

EXPLORING

There is not much that students can do to explore this field, since success as a certified financial planner comes only with training and years on the job. However, you can check out the financial planning information available on the Internet to familiarize yourself with the terms used in the industry. You should also take as many finance and business classes as possible. Talking to certified financial planners will also help you gather information on the field.

EMPLOYERS

Financial planners are employed by financial planning firms across the country. Many of these firms are small, perhaps employing two to 15 people, and most are located in urban areas. A smaller, but growing, number of financial planners are employed by corporations, banks, credit unions, mutual fund companies, insurance companies, accounting or law firms, colleges and universities, credit counseling organizations, and brokerage firms. In addition, many financial planners are self-employed.

STARTING OUT

Early in their careers, financial planners work for banks, mutual fund companies, or investment firms and usually receive extensive on-the-job training. The job will deal heavily with client-based and research activities. Financial planners may start their own business as they learn personal skills and build their client base. During their first few years, certified financial planners spend many hours analyzing documents, meeting with other advisers, and networking to find new clients.

ADVANCEMENT

Those who have not changed their career track in five years can expect to have established some solid, long-term relationships with clients. Measured success at this point will be the planners' service fees, which will be marked up considerably from when they started their careers.

Those who have worked in the industry for 10 years usually have many clients and a six-figure income. Experienced financial planners can also move into careers in investment banking, financial consulting, and financial analysis. Because people skills are also an integral part of being a financial planner, consulting, on both personal and corporate levels, is also an option. Many planners will find themselves attending business school, either to achieve a higher income or to switch to one of the aforementioned professions.

EARNINGS

There are several methods of compensation for financial planners. Fee-only means that compensation is earned entirely from fees from consultation, plan development, or investment management. These fees may be charged on an hourly or project basis depending on clients' needs or on a percentage of assets under management.

Commission-only compensation is received from the sale of financial products that clients agree to purchase to implement financial planning recommendations. There is no charge for advice or preparation of the financial plan. Fee-offset means that compensation received in the form of commission from the sale of financial products is offset against fees charged for the planning process. Combination fee/commission is a fee charged for consultation, advice, and financial plan preparation on an hourly, project, or percentage basis. Planners might also receive commissions from recommended products targeted to achieve goals and objectives. Some planners work on a salary basis for financial services institutions such as banks, credit unions, and other related organizations.

The mean annual gross income of certified financial planners was $283,079 in 2007, according to the *2007 Survey of Trends in the Financial Planning Industry* conducted by the College for Financial Planning. These incomes were earned from financial plan writing, product sales, consulting, and related activities.

The U.S. Department of Labor reports that financial planners earned a median annual salary of $66,120 in 2006. The most-experienced financial planners with the highest level of education earned more than $145,600, while the least-experienced financial planners earned less than $32,340.

Firms might also provide beginning financial planners with a steady income by paying a draw, which is a minimum salary based on the commission and fees the planner can be expected to earn.

Some financial planners receive vacation days, sick days, and health insurance, but that depends on whether they work for financial institutions or on their own.

WORK ENVIRONMENT

Most financial planners work by themselves in offices or at home. Others work in offices with other financial planners. Established financial planners usually work the same hours as others in the business community. Beginners who are seeking customers probably work longer hours. Many planners accommodate customers by meeting with them in the evenings and on weekends. They might spend a lot of time out of the office meeting with current and prospective clients, attending civic functions, and participating in trade association meetings.

OUTLOOK

The employment of financial planners is expected to grow rapidly in the future for a number of reasons. More funds should be available for investment, as the economy, personal income, and inherited wealth grow. Demographics will also play a role; as increasing numbers of baby boomers turn 50, demand will grow for retirement-related investments. Most people, in general, are likely to turn to financial planners for assistance with retirement planning. Individual saving and investing for retirement are expected to become more important, as many companies reduce pension benefits and switch from defined-benefit retirement plans to defined-contribution plans, which shift the investment responsibility from the company to the individual. Furthermore, a growing number of individual investors are expected to seek advice from financial planners regarding the increasing complexity and array of investment alternatives for assistance with estate planning.

Due to the highly competitive nature of financial planning, many beginners leave the field because they are not able to establish a sufficient clientele. Once established, however, planners have a strong attachment to their occupation because of high earning potential and considerable investment in training. Job opportunities should be best for mature individuals with successful work experience.

FOR MORE INFORMATION

For more information about financial education and the ChFC designation, contact
The American College
270 South Bryn Mawr Avenue
Bryn Mawr, PA 19010-2105
Tel: 888-263-7265
Email: studentservices@theamericancollege.edu
http://www.theamericancollege.edu/

To learn more about financial planning and to obtain a copy of the Guide to CFP Certification, *contact*
Certified Financial Planner Board of Standards
1670 Broadway, Suite 600
Denver, CO 80202-4809
Tel: 888-237-6275
Email: mail@CFPBoard.org
http://www.cfp.net

For information on financial planning, visit the FPA Web site.
Financial Planning Association (FPA)
4100 East Mississippi Avenue, Suite 400
Denver, CO 80246-3053

Tel: 800-322-4237
http://www.fpanet.org

For more information on fee-only financial advisers, contact
National Association of Personal Financial Advisors
3250 North Arlington Heights Road, Suite 109
Arlington Heights, IL 60004-1574
Tel: 800-366-2732
Email: info@napfa.org
http://www.napfa.org

Mathematicians

OVERVIEW

A *mathematician* solves or directs the solution of problems in higher mathematics, including algebra, geometry, number theory, logic, and topology. *Theoretical mathematicians* work with the relationships among mathematical forms and the underlying principles that can be applied to problems, including electronic data processing and military planning. *Applied mathematicians* develop the techniques and approaches to problem solving in the physical, biological, and social sciences. Approximately 2,500 mathematicians are employed in nonacademic settings in the United States.

HISTORY

Although mathematics may be considered a "pure" science—that is, one that may be studied for its own sake—math has often been applied to produce engineering and other scientific achievements. The non-Euclidean geometry developed by Bernard Riemann in 1854 seemed quite impractical at the time, yet some years later Albert Einstein used it as part of his work in the development of his theory of relativity. Einstein's theory similarly appeared to have no practical application at the time but later became the basis for work in nuclear energy.

Mathematics is a discipline used in the study of all sciences. In addition to contributing to the development of nuclear energy, mathematicians played important roles in the 20th century in the development of the automobile, the television, and space exploration. They have been instrumental in advancing research and experimental efforts in sociology, psychology, and education, among other fields. The development of space vehicles and electronic computers are but two examples that characterize the dynamic nature and increasing importance of mathematicians in the 21st century. Mathematicians, although working in one of the oldest and most basic of sciences, are always contributing new ideas.

THE JOB

There are two broad areas of opportunity in mathematics: theoretical and applied. In addition, mathematicians may choose to pursue a career in teaching. The duties performed, the processes involved, the work situations encountered, and the equipment used varies considerably, depending on the institutional or organizational setting.

Theoretical mathematicians deal with pure and abstract mathematical concepts rather than the practical application of such concepts to everyday problems. They might teach in a college or university or work in the research department of a business or government office. They are concerned with the advancement of mathematical knowledge, the logical development of mathematical systems, and the study and analysis of relationships among mathematical forms. "Pure" mathematicians focus their efforts mainly on problems dealing with mathematical principles and reasoning.

Applied mathematicians develop and apply mathematical knowledge to practical and research problems in the social, physical, life, and earth sciences. Business, industry, and government agencies such as the National Aeronautics and Space Administration (NASA) rely heavily on applied mathematicians, particularly for research and development programs. Therefore, it is necessary for these mathematicians to be knowledgeable about their employer's operations and products as well as their own field. Applied mathematicians work on problems ranging from the stability of rockets to the effects of new drugs on disease.

The applied and theoretical aspects of mathematicians' work are not always clearly separated. Some mathematicians, usually those dealing with the application of mathematics, may become involved in both aspects. In addition to having general knowledge about modern computing equipment, mathematicians need some basic experience in computer programming and operation because of the rapidly expanding reliance on computers.

Specialists in the field of applied mathematics include the following:

Computer applications engineers formulate mathematical models and develop computer systems to solve scientific and engineering problems.

Engineering analysts apply logical analysis to scientific, engineering, and other technical problems and convert them to mathematical terms to be solved by computers.

Operations research analysts employ mathematics to solve management and operational problems.

Weight analysts are concerned with weight, balance, loading, and operational functions of space vehicles, ships, aircraft, missiles, research instrumentation, and commercial and industrial products and systems. These mathematicians use computers to analyze weight factors and work with design engineers to coordinate their specifications with product development.

Mathematics teachers instruct students at the middle school and high school levels. In high school, they provide instruction in more complex mathematics such as algebra, geometry, trigonometry, precalculus, and calculus.

College mathematics professors provide instruction to future mathematicians and students in other disciplines. They often teach courses at various levels of difficulty. Professors usually spend less time in the classroom than high school teachers, but they may have many other responsibilities, including advising doctoral candidates, serving on university or mathematical organization committees, and reading mathematical books and journals. Some professors are also actively involved in research and in contributing to the development of the field; this often includes writing and submitting articles on their research to mathematical journals.

REQUIREMENTS

High School

To pursue a career as a mathematician, take all the math classes that are offered and can fit into your schedule. Meet with teachers to get as much insight as you can about doing well in the math courses offered at your school. These courses should include algebra, geometry, trigonometry, and calculus. If your school offers college prep courses, you may be able to study probability, statistics, and logic. Classes such as English composition and computer science are also important.

Summer Mathematics Programs

If you're interested in a career in mathematics, participating in a summer program offered by a college or university is a great way to learn more about the field. In these programs, you'll get the chance to be taught by top mathematics professors; learn how to solve mathematical problems; listen to lectures from experts; and interact with students just like you who are interested in mathematics. Most importantly, you'll get a chance to try out a career in mathematics before college. The following is a short list of summer mathematics programs for high school students:

Boston University (Boston, Mass.)
Program in Mathematics for Young Scientists
promys@bu.edu
http://www.promys.org

University of California–San Diego
MathZoom Summer Camp
info@MathZoom.com
http://www.mathzoom.com

University of Michigan (Ann Arbor, Mich.)
Michigan Math and Science Scholars
mmss@umich.edu
http://www.math.lsa.umich.edu/mmss

University of Minnesota (Minneapolis)
Institute of Technology Center for Educational Programs
itcep@umn.edu
http://www.itcep.umn.edu

University of Nebraska–Lincoln
All Girls/All Math Summer Camp for High School Girls

Postsecondary Training

Undergraduate mathematical study includes work in algebra, geometry, numerical analysis, topology, and statistics. Typical university courses include differential equations, linear algebra, advanced calculus, number theory, and theory and application of digital computers. In addition to these and other courses from which you may choose as a math major, you should also sample

agam@math.unl.edu
http://www.math.unl.edu/~agam

Ohio State University (Columbus, Ohio)
Ross Mathematics Program
ross@math.ohio-state.edu
http://www.math.ohio-state.edu/ross

Rutgers University–New Brunswick (Piscataway, N.J.)
Rutgers Young Scholars Program in Discrete Mathematics
toti@dimacs.rutgers.edu
http://dimacs.rutgers.edu/ysp

Stanford University (Stanford, Calif.)
Mathematics Camp
sommer@math.stanford.edu
http://math.stanford.edu/sumac

University of Texas–Dallas
AwesomeMath Summer Camp
titu@awesomemath.org
http://www.awesomemath.org

University of Utah–Salt Lake City
Summer Mathematics Program for High School Students
gardiner@math.utah.edu
http://www.math.utah.edu/hsp

University of Washington (Seattle)
Summer Institute for Mathematics
simuw@math.washington.edu
http://www.math.washington.edu/~simuw

For more summer mathematics programs, visit http://www.ams.org/
employment/mathcamps.html.

broadly in the humanities and the various social, physical, and life sciences.

With the exception of secondary school teaching and working for the federal government, the educational requirement for this profession is a doctoral degree in mathematics. A doctorate is necessary for most research and development positions as well as for college-level teaching. Approximately 200 colleges and universities offer a master's degree, and over 200 offer a Ph.D. in pure or applied mathematics.

Many colleges and universities require that if you major in math you must also take classes in another area related to math, such as computer science, engineering, physical science, or economics.

Certification or Licensing

If you're interested in teaching math in a public elementary or high school, you must be licensed. However, you usually do not need a license to teach in a private school. Requirements vary from state to state, although all states require that you have at least a bachelor's degree and have finished an approved teacher training program.

Government positions usually require that applicants take a civil service examination in addition to meeting certain specified requirements that vary according to the type and level of position.

Other Requirements

To be a mathematician requires abilities in abstract reasoning, analyzing, and interpreting mathematical ideas. Speed and accuracy with numbers are necessary skills, too. Finally, communication skills are important because you will often need to interact with others, many of whom may not have an extensive knowledge of mathematics.

EXPLORING

While in high school, you may wish to accelerate your studies by enrolling in summer session programs offering regular or elective mathematics courses. Some schools have specialized mathematics honors or advanced placement courses that are part of their regular summer or evening school programs. Ask your math teacher or guidance counselor if there are any mathematics competitions you can enter. Not only can they be fun, but competitions may also offer college scholarships as awards.

Summer and part-time employment with NASA or industrial firms can also provide you with valuable experience and offer the opportunity to test your knowledge, interests, abilities, and personal characteristics in a practical work setting.

EMPLOYERS

Mathematicians hold approximately 2,500 jobs in the federal and state government and in various private industries and business. An additional 53,000 work in mathematical faculty positions in colleges and universities.

In government, the Department of Defense and NASA are the main employers of mathematicians. Significant employers in industry include management and public relations, research and testing, aerospace, securities and commodities, and drug manufacturing companies. Other positions are held in such businesses as banks, insurance companies, securities and commodity exchanges, and public utilities.

STARTING OUT

Most college career services offices assist students in finding positions in business and industry upon graduation. Teaching positions in high schools are usually obtained by personal contacts through friends, relatives, or college professors or through college career services offices and by application and interviews. College and university assistantships, instructorships, and professorships often are obtained by departmental recommendations.

Positions in federal, state, and local governments are usually announced well in advance of the required civil service examination, and students can check for such notices on bulletin boards in their college career services offices or other locations, such as post offices and government buildings.

ADVANCEMENT

Numerous opportunities for advancement to higher-level positions or into related areas of employment are available to mathematicians. Promotions of mathematicians are generally made on the basis of advanced preparation, knowledge of a specific application, individual appraisal by a superior, or competitive examination.

Opportunities in related fields, such as statistics, accounting, actuarial work, and computers, allow mathematicians to change their profession, relocate geographically, or advance to better positions with higher salaries.

EARNINGS

Mathematicians' income varies with their level of training and the work setting in which they are employed. According to the U.S. Department of Labor, median annual earnings of mathematicians were $86,930 in 2006. Salaries ranged from less than $43,500 to more than $132,190. In 2005, the mean annual salary for mathematicians employed by the federal government was $88,194. Mathematical statisticians earned an average of $91,446 a year, and *cryptanalysts* (mathematicians who analyze and decipher coding systems to transmit military, political, financial, or law enforcement information) earned $70,774, according to the *Occupational Outlook Handbook*.

Mathematicians receive traditional benefits such as health insurance, vacation time, and sick leave. Teachers usually have more time off during semester breaks and summer vacations, although they still are occupied with tasks such as grading papers and advising students.

WORK ENVIRONMENT

The mathematician in industrial and government positions usually works a regular 40-hour week. Those who work in educational settings may have varied schedules. For both, the work environment is generally pleasant and typical of the modern, well-equipped office. The work may require long periods of close concentration. Professional mathematicians who work with or near computers usually work in air-conditioned buildings, as computers are extremely sensitive to temperature changes.

OUTLOOK

Overall employment of mathematicians is expected to decline through 2014. However, it is expected that there will be more jobs in applied mathematics (and related areas such as computer programming, operations research, and engineering design) than in theoretical research. Those who have a background in another field in addition to mathematics (such as computer science and software development, physics, engineering, or operations research) will have more opportunities. The Society for Industrial and Applied Mathematics predicts that opportunities will be good in the following emerging fields: computational biology and genomics, data-mining (including applications in astrophysics), neuroscience, materials science (including applications in aerospace, biology, electronics, and engineering), and computer animation and digital imaging.

Individuals with only a bachelor's degree in mathematics are not qualified for most mathematician jobs. However, those with a double major will have more opportunities. Holders of bachelor's or master's degrees in mathematics who also meet state certification requirements can find jobs as high school mathematics teachers. For mathematicians with a master's degree but no doctorate, jobs may be harder to find. Strong competition will exist for jobs in theoretical research. More openings should be available in applied areas, such as computer science and data processing.

FOR MORE INFORMATION

For a variety of useful resources about mathematics, including A Guide to Online Resources for High School Math Students, *visit the AMS Web site.*
American Mathematical Society (AMS)
201 Charles Street
Providence, RI 02904-2294
Tel: 800-321-4267
Email: ams@ams.org
http://www.ams.org

For information on opportunities for women in mathematics, contact
Association for Women in Mathematics
11240 Waples Mill Road, Suite 200
Fairfax, VA 22030-6078
Tel: 703-934-0163
Email: awm@awm-math.org
http://www.awm-math.org

For information on student competitions, contact
Mathematical Association of America
1529 18th Street, NW
Washington, DC 20036-1358
Tel: 800-741-9415
http://www.maa.org

For information on teaching careers in mathematics, contact
National Council of Teachers of Mathematics
1906 Association Drive
Reston, VA 20191-1502
Tel: 703-620-9840
http://www.nctm.org

For information on publications (including Thinking of a Career in Applied Mathematics?*), conferences, activity groups, and programs, contact*
> **Society for Industrial and Applied Mathematics**
> 3600 Market Street, 6th Floor
> Philadelphia, PA 19104-2688
> Tel: 215-382-9800
> http://www.siam.org

Mathematics Teachers

OVERVIEW

Mathematics teachers generally work with middle or high school students. They lecture, direct discussions, and test students' knowledge with exams, essays, and homework assignments. Teachers also develop teaching outlines and lesson plans, facilitate activities, keep class attendance records, and evaluate student progress.

HISTORY

Greek mathematicians in the sixth century B.C. helped to establish some of the basic laws and principles that govern mathematics today. They applied reason to write up proofs supporting geometric theorems. These theories were written in simple generalized form, using variables to represent "unknowns." The Pythagorean theorem ($a^2 + b^2 = c^2$) is an example of early mathematic discovery.

It was the Muslims who gave us the Arabic numbering system based on the number 10. This system was adopted by traveling traders and spread through Europe and eventually America. Principles of geometry and trigonometry were further developed and applied to navigation and surveying, resulting in great advances in these areas.

Today, new discoveries are as common in mathematics as new problems. The current wide scope of math has led to many advances in science, technology, and computer science in the last century.

QUICK FACTS

School Subjects
Computer science
Mathematics
Speech

Personal Skills
Helping/teaching
Technical/scientific

Work Environment
Primarily indoors
Primarily one location

Minimum Education Level
Bachelor's degree

Salary Range
$31,450 to $47,740 to
$76,100+

Certification or Licensing
Voluntary (certification)
Required for certain
positions (licensing)

Outlook
About as fast as the average

DOT
091

GOE
12.03.02, 12.03.03

NOC
4141

O*NET-SOC
25-2022.00, 25-2031.00

THE JOB

Many successful people credit their secondary school teachers with helping them discover their talents and abilities while guiding them into college, careers, and other endeavors. The primary responsibility of math teachers is to instruct students in grades seven through 12 in a specific math subject. Teachers may teach a traditional math subject, such as geometry, algebra, or trigonometry, or in an applied math area, such as information technology, statistics, or probability.

Many secondary schools are expanding their course offerings to better serve the individual interests of their students. "School-to-work" programs, which are vocational education programs designed for high school students and recent graduates, involve lab work and demonstrations to prepare students for highly technical jobs. Though they will likely be assigned to one specific level in a subject area, secondary school teachers may be required to teach multiple levels. For example, a secondary school mathematics teacher may teach algebra to a class of ninth graders one period and trigonometry to high school seniors the next.

In the classroom, math teachers rely on a variety of teaching methods. They spend a great deal of time lecturing, but they also facilitate student discussion and develop projects and activities to interest the students in the subject. They show films and videos, use computers and the Internet, and possibly even invite guest speakers. Aside from assigning the usual book problems, they may also assign presentations and other more creative projects to facilitate learning. Each individual area of math usually requires more than one teaching approach.

Outside the classroom, math teachers prepare lectures, lesson plans, and exams. They evaluate student work and calculate grades. In the process of planning their classes, math teachers read textbooks and workbooks to determine problem assignments; photocopy notes, articles, and other handouts; and develop grading policies. They also continue to study alternative and traditional teaching methods to hone their skills. Math teachers may prepare students for special events and conferences and prepare students for math competitions. Many also serve as sponsors to student organizations in their field, such as a math club. Secondary school teachers also have the opportunity for extracurricular work as athletic coaches or drama coaches, and they may monitor students during lunch, break times, and study halls. They may also accompany student groups on field days and to competitions and events. In addition, math teachers

A high school mathematics teacher discusses calculus equations with two of her students. *(James Marshall, The Image Works)*

attend faculty meetings, meet with parents, and may travel to state and national teacher conferences.

Mathematics teachers must keep their skills current and their teaching methods up to date. They may be required by state regulations to take continuing education courses and may have to pass periodic exams to prove their competency in the field. In a field as challenging as mathematics, teachers often explore their subject outside of the classroom as well, by conducting research or reading journals about the field.

REQUIREMENTS

High School

If you are interested in pursuing a career as a math teacher, prepare yourself by taking classes in algebra, geometry, trigonometry, and calculus in high school. If available, take advanced math classes in statistics, probability, and logic. Classes in speech and English composition courses are also helpful to develop your communication skills. You should also explore extracurricular activities that will further challenge your math skills, such as joining a math club. The more involved you are now, the better you'll look to future employers.

Postsecondary Training

There are more than 500 accredited teacher education programs in the United States. Most of these programs are designed to meet the certification requirements for the state in which they're located. Some states may require that you pass a test before being admitted to an education program. You may choose to major in mathematics while taking required education courses, or you may major in secondary education with a concentration in math. You'll probably have advisors in both math and education to help you select courses.

Practice teaching, also called student teaching, with a local school is usually required as part of the education program. To fulfill this requirement, you will be assigned to work with a full-time teacher for a period of time. During student teaching, you will observe the ways in which lessons are presented and the classroom is managed, learn how to keep records of such details as attendance and grades, and get actual experience in handling the class, both under supervision and alone.

Prospective high school teachers usually need 24 to 36 hours of college work in the subject they wish to teach. Some states require a master's degree; teachers with master's degrees can earn higher salaries. Private schools generally do not require an education degree.

Certification or Licensing

As a public school teacher, you must be licensed under regulations established by the department of education of the state in which you are teaching. Although requirements vary by state, most require a bachelor's degree and the completion of a state-approved education program. Certain courses and education credits must be fulfilled as part of these training programs, and some states may also require you to maintain a minimum grade point average or even obtain a master's degree in education before teaching. Technology training is also a part of many states' licensing requirements. Not all states require licensure for teachers in private or parochial schools.

When you have received your teaching degree, you may request that a transcript of your college record be sent to the licensure section of the state department of education. If you have met licensure requirements, you will receive a certificate and thus be eligible to teach in the public schools of the state. In some states, you may have to take a competency exam to prove your basic skills before teaching. If you move to another state, you will have to resubmit college transcripts as well as comply with any other regulations in the new state to be able to teach there.

Because of a current teacher shortage, many states offer alternative licensing programs for individuals with bachelor's degrees in a subject (such as math) who have not taken the required number of education courses. Individuals may begin teaching immediately under the supervision of a licensed teacher while taking education courses part time. After working for one or two years and taking the required courses, they can earn a license.

The National Board for Professional Teaching Standards offers voluntary certification for teachers. To earn certification, individuals must pass a written assessment evaluating their teaching knowledge. All states recognize national certification and may grant higher salaries and promotions to those who obtain it.

Other Requirements

To succeed as a math teacher, not only will you need to meet all the educational and licensure requirements, but you should also have the right personality for the job. You will need respect for young people and a genuine interest in their success in life. In teaching, patience is most certainly a virtue; adolescence can be a troubling time for children, and these troubles often affect behavior and classroom performance. You may find yourself frustrated and discouraged by students' reactions or lack of response to you as their teacher. During these times, it is important to keep a level head and be patient as you try to connect with and educate them.

You will be working with students who are at very impressionable ages; you should serve as a good role model. You should also be well organized, as you'll have to keep track of the work and progress of a number of different students.

EXPLORING

By attending your own high school math classes, you have already gained a good sense of the daily work of a math teacher. But the requirements of a teacher extend far beyond the classroom, so ask to spend some time with one of your teachers after school. Ask about their job, how they prepared for their career, and look at lecture notes and record-keeping procedures.

To get some direct teaching experience, volunteer for a peer tutoring program. Other teaching opportunities outside your school may exist in your community; look into coaching an athletic team at the YMCA, counseling at a summer camp, teaching a math course at a community center, or assisting with a community theater production.

Regardless of what subject you teach, gaining this outside experience will give you a taste of what it feels like to instruct others.

Consider joining the Junior Engineering Technical Society (JETS). JETS promotes learning in mathematics, engineering, science, and technology. Visit its Web site at http://www.jets.org. You may also find it helpful to read publications about this field and visit Web sites such as S.O.S. Mathematics (http://www.sosmath.com) and The Math Forum (http://www.mathforum.org).

EMPLOYERS

Math teachers are needed at middle, junior high, and high schools, including parochial schools, juvenile detention centers, vocational schools, and technical schools. Some Montessori schools are also expanding to include more advanced courses. Though rural areas maintain some schools, most institutions are in towns and cities. Teachers can also find opportunities in "charter" schools, which are smaller, deregulated schools that receive public funding.

STARTING OUT

After completing the teacher certification process, including your months of student teaching, you should work with your college's career services office to find a full-time position. In some states, the departments of education maintain listings of job openings. In addition, many schools advertise teaching positions in the classified sections of the state's major newspapers. You may also directly contact principals and superintendents of the schools in which you would like to work. While waiting for full-time work, you can work as a substitute teacher. Substituting will give you more than a paycheck; you will gain worthwhile teaching experience and learn about different school systems as a sub. In some school districts, you may be able to substitute full time.

ADVANCEMENT

Most math teachers advance in the sense that they become more expert in the job that they have chosen. There is usually an increase in salary as teachers acquire years of experience. Additional training or study can also bring an increase in salary.

Teachers with administrative ability and an interest in administrative work may advance to the position of principal. Others work into supervisory positions or as assistants, helping teachers find appropriate instructional materials and develop certain phases of their courses of study. Teachers may decide to focus their careers more on education than on the subject they teach by moving into teacher education at a college or university. For most of these positions, a master's degree in education is required. Some teachers also make lateral moves into other education-related positions such as school counselor or resource room teacher.

EARNINGS

Most teachers are contracted to work nine months out of the year, though some contracts are made for a full 12 months. When regular school is not in session, teachers are usually expected to conduct summer teaching, planning, or other school-related work.

According to the U.S. Department of Labor, the median annual salary for secondary school teachers was $47,740 in 2006. The lowest 10 percent earned less than $31,760, and the highest 10 percent made $76,100 or more annually. The median annual salary of middle school teachers was $46,300 in 2006. The lowest paid 10 percent of these teachers earned less than $31,450, and the top 10 percent made $73,350 or more per year.

Teachers can also supplement their earnings through teaching summer classes, coaching sports, sponsoring a club, or other extra-curricular work. Unions such as the American Federation of Teachers and the National Education Association negotiate with schools over contract conditions such as wages, hours, and benefits. Depending on the state, teachers usually receive a retirement plan, sick leave, and health and life insurance. Some systems grant teachers sabbatical leave.

WORK ENVIRONMENT

Although the job of the math teacher is not physically strenuous, it can be tiring and trying. Teachers must stand for many hours each day, do a lot of talking, show energy and enthusiasm, and handle discipline problems. Despite this often trying task, they also have the reward of guiding students in making decisions about their lives and futures.

Math teachers work under generally pleasant conditions, though some older schools may have poor heating and electrical systems. Though violence in schools has decreased in recent years, media coverage of the violence has increased along with student fears. In most schools, students are prepared to learn and to perform the work that's required of them. But in some schools, students may be dealing with gangs, drugs, poverty, and other problems, so the environment can be tense and emotional.

School hours are generally 8:00 A.M. to 3:00 P.M., but teachers work more than 40 hours a week. Outside the classroom, they spend a lot of time preparing for classes, grading papers, and directing extracurricular activities. Some work evenings and weekends, coaching school teams or tutoring students. Many teachers enroll in master's or doctoral programs and take evening and summer courses to continue their education.

OUTLOOK

Employment for teachers is predicted to grow at an average rate through 2014, according to the U.S. Department of Labor. Many schools are in short supply of educators, partly due to the large number of teachers expected to retire. As a result, school systems are competing for teachers in many locations, using bonuses and higher pay to lure the most qualified.

The U.S. Department of Education predicts that 180,000 more secondary teachers will be needed by 2012 to meet rising enrollments and to replace the large number of retiring teachers. Math teachers, in particular, are in short supply, especially in large cities. The National Education Association believes this will be a challenge because of the low salaries that are paid to secondary school teachers. Higher salaries will be necessary to attract new teachers and retain experienced ones, along with other changes such as smaller classroom sizes and safer schools. Other challenges for the profession involve attracting more men into teaching. The percentage of male teachers at this level continues to decline.

FOR MORE INFORMATION

For information about careers and current issues affecting teachers, contact
American Federation of Teachers
555 New Jersey Avenue, NW
Washington, DC 20001-2029
Tel: 202-879-4400
http://www.aft.org

For information on student competitions, contact
Mathematical Association of America
1529 18th Street, NW

Washington, DC 20036-1358
Tel: 800-741-9415
http://www.maa.org

For information on certification, contact
National Board for Professional Teaching Standards
1525 Wilson Boulevard, Suite 500
Arlington, VA 22209-2451
Tel: 800-228-3224
http://www.nbpts.org

For information on accredited teacher education programs, contact
National Council for Accreditation of Teacher Education
2010 Massachusetts Avenue, NW, Suite 500
Washington, DC 20036-1023
Tel: 202-466-7496
Email: ncate@ncate.org
http://www.ncate.org

For information on teaching careers in mathematics, contact
National Council of Teachers of Mathematics
1906 Association Drive
Reston, VA 20191-1502
Tel: 703-620-9840
http://www.nctm.org

For information on public education, contact
National Education Association
1201 16th Street, NW
Washington, DC 20036-3290
Tel: 202-833-4000
http://www.nea.org

Operations Research Analysts

QUICK FACTS

School Subjects
Computer science
Mathematics

Personal Skills
Communication/ideas
Technical/scientific

Work Environment
Primarily indoors
Primarily one location

Minimum Education Level
Master's degree

Salary Range
$38,760 to $64,650 to
$108,290+

Certification or Licensing
None available

Outlook
More slowly than the average

DOT
020

GOE
02.06.02

NOC
2161

O*NET-SOC
15-2031.00

OVERVIEW

Operations research analysts work in the field of applied mathematics. They convert management and operational data into a mathematical model and solve problems using analytical and mathematical techniques. They might help an airline streamline its service, a retail chain determine peak shopping hours, or a restaurant decide how to price the items on its menu. By preparing the business problem in mathematical terms, they are able to find cost-effective solutions. Operations research analysts hold approximately 58,000 jobs in the United States.

HISTORY

Although mathematics may be considered a "pure" science (one studied for its own sake), this abstract knowledge has often been applied to produce engineering and other scientific achievements. The non-Euclidean geometry developed by Bernard Riemann in 1854, for example, seemed quite impractical at the time, yet some years later Albert Einstein used it as part of his work in the development of the theory of relativity.

In the last several decades, operations research analysts and other applied mathematicians have begun to use mathematical formulas while conducting research in such fields as business management. The techniques they use generally revolve around the use of a set of mathematical equations that explain how things happen within a specified business environment. They develop models that examine the mathematical relationships between different managerial concerns, such as inventory control and distribution systems.

THE JOB

Operations research analysts apply mathematics to everyday situations and problems. They find practical applications for theoretical principles. They often work as part of a research team consisting of other mathematicians and engineers, and they frequently use data-processing equipment in their research. They prepare written and oral reports of their findings for upper-management officials.

These analysts can be found in a variety of industries and research settings, especially in engineering and the physical sciences. The business problems they evaluate and their specific job responsibilities vary according to the employer. For example, an analyst for a retail store might design store layouts, select the best store location, and analyze customer characteristics. An analyst for a hospital might study patient flow and forecast demand for new medical services. Some analysts specialize in one type of application; others are generalists.

Company managers usually begin the process by describing a business problem to the analyst. For example, a bank president wants to improve the overall check-processing procedure and know which type of personnel should handle specific job responsibilities. First the analyst selects the most practical and accurate method of computing all the data. He or she may use algebra, trigonometry, vector analysis, or calculus to simplify raw data into manageable terms.

After analysts define the problem, they prepare charts, tables, and diagrams to describe the flow of information or products. They use mathematical methods as analytical tools as well as various other techniques, such as cost accounting and sampling. Analysts also talk to other company personnel to understand the working network. In the end, they create a mathematical model or set of equations that explain how things happen within the represented system.

Mathematical models are simplified representations that enable the analyst to break down systems into their component parts, assign numerical values to each component, and examine the mathematical relationships between them. For example, a model for the check-processing procedure might include an analysis of the network flow: a process that identifies and defines the workers that handle each check that enters the bank. The model would also consider the number of checks processed daily, the current error rate in the process, and the cost to the bank of operating with the current procedure.

Two types of computerized models often used by operations research analysts include simulation and linear programming. Analysts must be able not only to use these programs, but also to work with computer programmers to write new programs. Analysts may need to alter existing models to determine what will happen to the system under different sets of circumstances. Some problems may have more than one useful approach. Analysts usually experiment with several models to ensure that the most efficient one is being used.

Analysts then interpret their results and translate them into terms understandable to management. They usually transcribe the data into equations, flowcharts, graphs, or other media. It is then up to management officials to implement a decision or ask research analysts to develop other options. After a final decision is made, analysts work with staff to implement the proposed solution. The entire process, from beginning to end, may last only a few hours or may take as long as a year.

REQUIREMENTS

High School

A strong background in and aptitude for mathematics, science, or engineering is necessary if you are interested in a career as an operations research analyst. While in high school, take college preparatory courses, such as English, history, science, and as many mathematics and statistics courses as possible. Because the computer is an important tool for the research analyst, you should also take any available computer programming courses.

Postsecondary Training

Most employers require that applicants have a master's degree in operations research, mathematics, business administration, computer science, engineering, business, information systems, or management science to be considered for employment. Most aspiring operations research analysts first earn a bachelor's degree in computer science or a quantitative discipline, such as mathematics, statistics, or economics, as preparation for graduate study. An increasing number of employers look for graduates with dual degrees in operations research and computer science.

Core college classes include calculus, advanced calculus, linear algebra, statistics, and computers. Analysts take courses in applied mathematics, such as linear and nonlinear programming, discreet optimization, and graph theory.

Increasing specialization in the field means that employers will seek out analysts who are trained to handle certain types of problems. For example, someone with a background in business administration might be asked to handle problems dealing with financial data or personnel scheduling.

Other Requirements

Operations research analysts work with complex formulas and equations. However, it's not enough for them just to be good with numbers. Analysts should truly enjoy math and all its applications.

Diligence and attention to detail are extremely important, as is patience. Communication skills are also important because all research findings must be fully explained, both in written reports and during meetings with management officials. In addition, positions with the federal government usually require the applicant to pass a civil service examination.

EXPLORING

Because work in this field requires advanced study, it is hard to get hands-on experience while in high school. However, part-time work with a bank or insurance company that has an in-house operations research department can give you some exposure to the career. You might also consider enrolling in special summer sessions or advanced placement mathematics courses to further develop your knowledge of mathematics.

In addition to job and school exploration, talk with professionals already working in the field to get an accurate picture of the rewards and responsibilities involved with the job.

EMPLOYERS

There are approximately 58,000 operations research analysts working in the United States. Most find jobs in private industry. Telecommunication companies, aerospace manufacturers, computer systems design firms, financial institutions, insurance carriers, and engineering and management services firms are among some of the largest employers. Private consulting firms also frequently hire these analysts because businesses of all kinds are relying more and more on analysts' services to help them streamline their production methods and provide the most cost-efficient service possible. The federal government, especially the U.S. Department of Defense, employs many operations research analysts.

STARTING OUT

College career services counselors usually help qualified graduates find business and industry opportunities. College graduates can also directly contact appropriate companies on their own to inquire about job opportunities.

New employees usually have several months of on-the-job training in which they learn about the individual company's systems. Entry-level employees work closely with experienced personnel during this period.

ADVANCEMENT

Operations research analysts have numerous opportunities for advancement to higher-level management positions or into related areas of employment. Skilled analysts may be promoted to the head of an operations research staff or may move to another upper-level management position within a firm. They may also choose to move to a larger company. Promotions usually go to those analysts who have computer skills, technical experience, and the ability to manage people and organize projects. Some successful analysts with a great deal of experience may choose to open their own consulting companies. Those with the proper education and experience may also move into a related field, such as statistics or actuarial work.

EARNINGS

Earnings vary based on experience, type of job, and geographic location. According to the U.S. Department of Labor, the median annual salary of operations research analysts was $64,650 in 2006. The lowest paid 10 percent earned less than $38,760; the highest paid earned more than $108,290.

Analysts working for the federal government earned a mean salary of $94,610 in 2006. Earnings in private industry varied. In computer systems design and related services, operations research analysts earned a mean salary of $75,700 a year; in management and technical consulting services, $74,690; and in the insurance industry, $60,180.

WORK ENVIRONMENT

Analysts typically work a regular 40-hour week in a comfortable office setting with computers close at hand. They may work overtime if a project is facing a deadline.

The work is sedentary in nature and may require long periods of close concentration on mathematical formulas and their application to specific management concerns.

OUTLOOK

According to the *Occupational Outlook Handbook,* growth within the field of operations research is predicted to be slower than the average rate for all occupations through 2014. Despite slow growth, opportunities in operations research should still be good. During slower and hence more competitive economic periods, analysts are needed to help increase levels of productivity or lower operation costs.

In addition, the number of positions created by people leaving the occupation should exceed the number of new qualified candidates. Few new job openings in the field will be listed under the title "operations research analyst." Increasingly, new jobs will be listed under job titles such as management analyst, computer scientist, or systems analyst. Job prospects will be the best for those with a master's or Ph.D. in operations research or a related field.

FOR MORE INFORMATION

For more information on career and employment opportunities, contact

American Mathematical Society
201 Charles Street
Providence, RI 02904-2294
Tel: 800-321-4267
Email: ams@ams.org
http://www.ams.org

For information on opportunities for women in the mathematical sciences, contact

Association for Women in Mathematics
11240 Waples Mill Road, Suite 200
Fairfax, VA 22030-6078
Tel: 703-934-0163
Email: awm@awm-math.org
http://www.awm-math.org

For information on student competitions, contact

Mathematical Association of America
1529 18th Street, NW

Washington, DC 20036-1358
Tel: 800-741-9415
http://www.maa.org

For information on careers and educational programs, contact
Institute for Operations Research and the Management Sciences
7240 Parkway Drive, Suite 310
Hanover, MD 21076-1310
Tel: 800-446-3676
Email: informs@informs.org
http://www.informs.org

For information on careers in the military and at the U.S. Department of Defense, contact
Military Operations Research Society
1703 North Beauregard Street, Suite 450
Alexandria, VA 22311-1745
Tel: 703-933-9070
Email: morsoffice@mors.org
http://www.mors.org

For information on careers, contact
Society for Industrial and Applied Mathematics
3600 Market Street, 6th Floor
Philadelphia, PA 19104-2688
Tel: 215-382-9800
http://www.siam.org

Physicists

OVERVIEW

Physics is a science dealing with the interaction of matter and energy. *Physicists* study the behavior and structure of matter, the ways that energy is generated and transferred, and the relationships between matter and energy. They perform experiments and analyze the products or results of those experiments. They may teach, oversee scientific projects, or act as consultants in a laboratory. They investigate and attempt to understand the fundamental laws of nature and how these laws may be formulated and put to use. There are approximately 16,000 physicists and astronomers (a subfield of physics) employed in the United States.

HISTORY

About 330 B.C., when Aristotle was writing *Physics*, physics was considered a branch of philosophy. It wasn't until over a thousand years later that physics evolved into a mathematically based science.

Galileo is often called the first modern physicist. His most famous experiment, in which he dropped a 10-pound weight and a one-pound weight from the Leaning Tower of Pisa, proved that all weights fall at the same speed. Both weights hit the ground simultaneously. Galileo's later work in astronomy, with the aid of a telescope, proved that the moon was not smooth. Through mathematical calculations, he proved that the moon reflects the light of the Sun.

In the four centuries since Galileo demonstrated the value of conducting experiments to determine whether or not scientific theory may be valid, scholars have made great strides. Michael Faraday conducted experiments that made the modern age of electricity possible. A generation later, Thomas Edison took advantage of his studies to produce more than a thousand inventions, including the incandescent light and the motion picture. In 1897, Sir Joseph John (J.J.) Thompson proved the existence of the electron. A year later, Marie Curie and Pierre Curie discovered radium. Niels Bohr proposed a theory of atomic structure; Albert Einstein developed the mathematical theories that have led us into the atomic age.

Physicists have made great progress in recent years in probing the depths of the ocean and conducting research in nuclear energy, communications, and aerospace.

THE JOB

Physics is the most comprehensive of the natural sciences because it includes the behavior of all kinds of matter from the smallest particles to the largest galaxies.

Basic, or pure, physics is a study of the behavior of the universe and is organized into a series of related laws. Basic physics can be studied from two points of view, experimental and theoretical. A physicist may work from one or both of these points of view. The *experimental physicist* performs experiments to gather information. The results of the experiments may support or contradict existing theories or establish new ideas where no theories existed before.

The *theoretical physicist* constructs theories to explain experimental results. If the theories are to stand the test of time, they must also predict the results of future experiments. Both the experimental physicist and the theoretical physicist try to extend the limits of what is known.

Not all physicists are concerned with testing or developing new theories. *Applied physicists* develop useful devices and procedures and may hold alternative job titles. Various types of engineers, such as electrical and mechanical engineers, are trained in physics. Applied physics and engineering have led to the development of such devices as television sets, airplanes, washing machines, satellites, and elevators.

Physicists rely heavily on mathematics. Mathematical statements are more precise than statements in words alone. Moreover, the results of experiments can be accurately compared with the various theories only when mathematical techniques are used.

The various laws of physics attempt to explain the behavior of nature in a simple and general way. Even the most accepted laws of physics, however, are subject to change. Physicists continually subject the laws of physics to new tests to see if, under new conditions, they still hold true. If they do not hold true, changes must be made in the laws, or entirely new theories must be proposed.

At the beginning of the 20th century, the laws of physics were tested extensively and found to be too narrow to explain many of the new discoveries. A new body of theories was needed. The older body of laws is called classical physics; the new is called modern physics.

Classical physics is usually divided into several branches, each of which deals with a group of related phenomena. *Mechanics* is the study of forces and their effect on matter. *Hydromechanics* studies the mechanics of liquids and gases. *Optics* is the study of the behavior of light. Physicists in this field study such things as lasers, liquid crystal displays, or light-emitting diodes. *Thermodynamics* is the study of heat. *Acoustics* is the study of sound, such as in recording studio acoustics, underwater sound waves, and electroacoustical devices such as loudspeakers. The study of electricity and magnetism also forms a branch of classical physics. Research in this area includes microwave propagation, the magnetic properties of matter, and electrical devices for science and industry.

Modern physics is also broken up into various fields of study. *Atomic physics* is the study of the structure of atoms and the behavior of electrons, one of the kinds of particles that make up the atom. *Nuclear physics* is the study of the nucleus, or center, of the atom and of the forces that hold the nucleus together. *High-energy physics,* or *particle physics,* is the study of the production of subatomic particles from other particles and energy. The characteristics of these various particles are studied using particle accelerators, popularly called atom smashers.

Solid-state physics is the study of the behavior of solids, particularly crystalline solids. Cryogenic, or low-temperature, techniques are often used in research into the solid state. Research in solid-state physics has produced transistors, integrated circuits, and masers that have improved computers, radios, televisions, and navigation and guidance systems for satellites. *Plasma physics* is the study of the properties of highly ionized gases. Physicists in this field are concerned with the generation of thermonuclear power.

Although biology and geology are separate sciences in their own right, the concepts of physics can also be applied directly to them. Where this application has been made, a new series of sciences has developed. To separate them from their parent sciences, they are known by such names as *biophysics* (the physics of living things) and *geophysics* (the physics of the earth). Similarly, the sciences of chemistry and physics sometimes overlap in subject matter as

Study of Physics Growing in Popularity

The study of physics is becoming more popular at both the high school and college levels, according to the American Institute of Physics. According to recent data from the institute:

- More than 30 percent of high school seniors have taken physics classes—the highest percentage ever recorded.

- The percentage of women and minorities who take high school physics classes is also rising. Females make up 47 percent of high school physics students today—an increase of 8 percent from 1987. African Americans and Hispanic Americans make up 23 and 24 percent, respectively, of all students taking high school physics classes. Only 10 percent of African Americans and Hispanic Americans took high school physics classes in 1990.

- The number of students earning physics bachelor's degrees has increased by 31 percent since 2000.

- Students who earn a bachelor's degree in physics are much more likely to pursue advanced degrees than those who have earned non-physics bachelor's degrees.

well as in viewpoint and procedure, creating *physical chemistry*. In *astrophysics*, the techniques of physics are applied to astronomical observations to determine the properties of celestial objects.

Most physicists are engaged in research, and some combine their research with teaching at the university level. Some physicists are employed in industries, such as petroleum, communications, manufacturing, and medicine.

REQUIREMENTS

High School

If you are interested in becoming a physicist, take college preparatory courses. You should take as much mathematics as is offered in your school as well as explore as many of the sciences as possible. English skills are important, as you must write up your results, communicate with other scientists, and lecture on your findings. In addition, get as much experience as possible working with computers.

Postsecondary Training

Physicists may have one, two, or three degrees. Physicists at the doctoral level command the jobs with the greatest responsibility, such as jobs in basic research and development. Those at the master's level often work in manufacturing or applied research. Those with a bachelor's degree face the most competition and generally work as technicians in engineering, software development, or other scientific areas.

Some employers in industry are attracted to those with a broad scientific background. With a bachelor's degree in physics or a related science, you may be hired with the intention of being trained on the job in a specialty area. As you develop competency in the special field, you may then consider returning to graduate school to concentrate your study in this particular field.

In addition, some teaching opportunities are available to those with bachelor's degrees at the primary and secondary school level. However, in order to teach at the college level (and even at some secondary schools), you will need an advanced degree. While a master's degree may be acceptable to teach at a junior college, most universities require that professors have their doctorates. Those with a master's degree may obtain a job as an assistant in a physics department in a university while working toward a Ph.D. in physics.

More than 510 colleges and universities offer a bachelor's degree in physics, and about 253 schools offer master's and doctoral programs. The American Institute of Physics provides a list of graduate institutions; see the end of this article for contact information.

Certification or Licensing

Those who plan to teach at the secondary school level may be able to obtain a teaching position with a bachelor's degree if they also meet the certification requirements for teaching (established by the department of education in each state). Because different states have different certification requirements, undergraduates should research the requirements for the state in which they hope to teach.

Other Requirements

Physicists are detail oriented and precise. They must have patience and perseverance and be self-motivated. Physicists should be able to work alone or on research teams.

EXPLORING

If you are interested in a job in physics, talk with your science teachers and research careers in the school library. See if your school offers science clubs, such as a physics or astronomy club, to get involved with others who hold the same interests as you. Participation in science fair projects will give you invaluable insight into theory, experimentation, and the scientific process. If your school does not sponsor science fairs, you may find fairs sponsored by your school district, state, or a science society.

EMPLOYERS

Approximately 16,000 physicists and astronomers work in the United States, most of them in industry, in research and development laboratories, and in teaching. Twenty-five percent of all physicists work for the federal government, mostly in the Department of Defense. Other government physicists work in the Departments of Energy, Health and Human Services, and Commerce, and for the National Aeronautics and Space Administration. Those working in industry jobs may hold a job title other than physicist, such as computer programmer, engineer, or systems developer.

STARTING OUT

The career services office of the college or university from which you obtain a degree will often have listings of jobs available. In addition, many industries send personnel interviewers to college campuses with physics programs to seek out and talk to students who are about to receive degrees. Students should also attend industry, career, and science fairs to find out about job openings and interview opportunities.

Those who are interested in teaching in public schools should apply to several school systems in which they may want to work. Some of the larger school systems also send personnel interviewers to campuses to talk with students who are about to receive degrees in science and who also have acquired the necessary courses in education.

Teaching jobs in universities are often obtained either through the contacts of the student's own faculty members in the degree program or through the career services office of the university.

Jobs with government agencies require individuals to first pass a civil service examination. For more information on federal employment, check out the USA Jobs Web site, http://www.usajobs.opm.gov.

ADVANCEMENT

High school physics teachers can advance in salary and responsibility as they acquire experience. Their advancement is also likely to be facilitated by attaining advanced degrees. The college or university teacher can advance from assistant to full professor and perhaps to head of the department. Higher rank also carries with it additional income and responsibilities.

The research physicist employed by a university advances by handling more responsibility for planning and conducting research programs. Salaries should also increase with experience in research over a period of years.

Physicists in federal government agencies advance in rank and salary as they gain experience. They may reach top positions in which they are asked to make decisions vital to the defense effort or to the safety and welfare of the country.

Scientists employed by industry are usually the highest paid in the profession and with experience can advance to research director positions.

EARNINGS

According to the U.S. Department of Labor, the median salary for physicists was $94,240 in 2006. The lowest paid 10 percent earned $52,070 or less; the highest 10 percent earned $143,570 or more. Physicists employed by the federal government had mean earnings of $102,920 in 2006.

In 2004, median salaries for members of the American Institute of Physics ranged from $72,000 for those with a bachelor's degree to $104,000 for those with a doctorate.

As highly trained and respected scientists, physicists usually receive excellent benefits packages, including health plans, vacation and sick leave, and other benefits.

WORK ENVIRONMENT

Most physicists work a 40-hour week under pleasant circumstances. Laboratories are usually well equipped, clean, well lighted, temperature controlled, and functional. Adequate safety measures are taken when there is any sort of physical hazard involved in the work. Often, groups of scientists work together as a team so closely that their association may last over a period of many years.

Physicists who teach at the high school, college, or university level have the added benefit of the academic calendar, which gives them ample time away from teaching and meeting with students in order to pursue their own research, studies, or travel.

OUTLOOK

According to the *Occupational Outlook Handbook,* employment for physicists should grow more slowly than the average for all occupations through 2014. Although increases in government research, particularly in the Departments of Defense and Energy, as well as in physics-related research in the private sector, will create more opportunities for physicists, there will be stiff competition among Ph.D. holders for basic positions. The need to replace retiring workers will account for almost all new job openings.

Private industry budgets for research and development will continue to grow, but many laboratories are expected to reduce their physics-based research to focus on product and software development and applied or manufacturing research. Opportunities will exist for physicists who work with computer technology, information technology, semiconductor technology, and other applied sciences.

Job candidates with doctoral degrees have the best outlook for finding work. Graduates with bachelor's degrees are generally underqualified for most physicist jobs. They may find better employment opportunities as engineers, technicians, or computer specialists. With a suitable background in education, they may teach physics at the high school level.

FOR MORE INFORMATION

For employment statistics and information on jobs and career planning, contact
American Institute of Physics
One Physics Ellipse
College Park, MD 20740-3843
Tel: 301-209-3100
http://www.aip.org

For information on educational requirements and careers, contact
American Physical Society
One Physics Ellipse
College Park, MD 20740-3844
Tel: 301-209-3200
http://www.aps.org

Fermilab offers internships, learning and employment opportunities, and general information about its laboratory. For more information, contact

Fermi National Accelerator Laboratory
PO Box 500
Batavia, IL 60510-0500
Tel: 630-840-3000
http://www.fnal.gov

*For career information and employment opportunities in Canada,
contact*
Canadian Association of Physicists
University of Ottawa
150 Louis Pasteur Avenue
Suite 112, MacDonald Building
Ottawa, ON K1N 6N5 Canada
Tel: 613-562-5614
Email: cap@physics.uottawa.ca
http://www.cap.ca

Sports Statisticians

QUICK FACTS

School Subjects
Computer science
Mathematics

Personal Skills
Leadership/management

Work Environment
Indoors and outdoors
Primarily multiple locations

Minimum Education Level
High school diploma

Salary Range
$5,000 to $35,000 to
$100,000

Certification or Licensing
None available

Outlook
About as fast as the average

DOT
020

GOE
11.01.02

NOC
2161

O*NET-SOC
15-2041.00

OVERVIEW

Sports statisticians compute and record the statistics relating to a particular sports event, game, or competition, or the accomplishments of a team or single athlete during competition. They do this manually or by using calculators or computers. There are approximately 19,000 statisticians in the United States, but sports statisticians make up only a very small portion of this group.

HISTORY

Statistics is a relatively new science relating to the collection and interpretation of data. Ancient record keeping can be traced back to the Old Testament and to population records compiled by the Babylonians and the Romans. Formal population studies in a scientific sense, however, were only begun early in the 19th century in the United States and certain European countries. The motivation for such statistics was primarily to promote efficient bureaucracies, but statistical studies were conducted to try to solve other problems in fields as diverse as social science, biology, and physics.

In the late 19th century, British statistician Sir Ronald Aylmer Fisher began his investigations on experimental designs, randomization, and mathematical statistics. Fisher and others developed small-sample statistical techniques and methods, such as the analysis of variance and covariance. His contributions are regarded by many as the origin of modern statistics. Since then, the field of statistics has grown rapidly, and statistics are used in nearly every area of study, from agriculture to health science to sports.

Sports fans, athletes, and coaches have kept informal records of the best and worst performances since before organized sports began. Early in the 19th century, as the rules and regulations of different sports began to be organized by official gaming associations, the importance of official record keeping was recognized. Soon, statistics were not only a vital resource when deciding which records were set or broken, but they also were being used to help determine the outcome of specific plays. For example, during a basketball game the referee asks the official scorer and statistician how many time-outs the home team has already taken or how many fouls a certain player has received.

Once, the statistician sat in the bleachers or on the bench, marking up a scoring book with slashes and checks to indicate runs, goals, fouls, and so on. Later, the statistician would tally up the various totals, computing team averages as well as individual play averages. Today, professional sports associations and leagues have highly sophisticated computers and programs that instantly tally the totals, averages, and percentages at the touch of a button.

THE JOB

Sports statisticians compute and record the statistics relating to a particular sports event, game, or competition, or the accomplishments of a team or single athlete during competition. They use their own knowledge of basic math and algebraic formulas, alone or in combination with calculators and computers, to calculate the statistics related to a particular sport or athlete.

Most high school, college, and professional team sports have an *official scorer* or *official statistician* who attends every home game and sits courtside, at what is called the scorer's table. The *team statistician* running stats at a basketball game, for example, keeps track of the score, the number of time-outs, and specific calls made by the referees, such as team and player fouls. The statistician is also referred to as the official scorer because if any item on the scoreboard is questioned by a referee, one of the coaches, or another game official, the individual who ultimately has the power to determine the outcome is the statistician.

Many statisticians still work by hand with a special notebook for recording the game statistics. As each play and call occurs in the game, the statistician records the play or call in a particular column or row of the stat book. Later, the statistician will make a tally of the total number of player errors, rebounds, assists, goals, etc. He or she can determine such statistics as the average number of rebounds in a quarter or per game. The statistician uses the same, predetermined algebraic formulas to compute the statistics for a single athlete or an entire team. Usually, the statistician keeps the stats, for both the home team and the visiting team, by individual. At the end of the game, the statistician can then provide both coaches and teams with specific information on their respective play during the game.

Other statisticians use computers with specialized software programs that automatically compute the player and team statistics. Most professional athletic teams have both a manual scorer and one or more individuals keeping statistics with the league- or association-sponsored statistics program. For example, both the National Basketball Association (NBA) and the National Football League (NFL) have computerized statistics programs that are used throughout the league or association. These programs, created by independent, private companies, allow each team to choose the statisticians who will run the system, while ensuring that the statistics systems used will be universal. One such company, SuperStats, created the computerized system for the NFL. In many cases, the computer system that calculates the different statistics also controls the different scoreboards in the arena or stadium and can quickly and efficiently produce flash and quarter stats for the teams, coaching staff, and various members of the media.

In professional team sports, the home team is responsible for making certain an official scorer/statistician is in attendance at all home games. The away or visiting team may have its own statistician or staff of statisticians, but the individual responsible for the official scores and stats is hired by the home team, and this is usually the same person throughout an entire season.

Statisticians begin work by arriving at the arena or stadium in plenty of time to set up, greet the officials, peruse any announcements or press releases from the public relations offices of the home or visiting team, and get the starting lineups from both the home and visiting team coaches. Statisticians who work with computer equipment may arrive even earlier to set up their equipment and make sure the system is up and running well in advance of game time.

Once the game begins, statisticians quite literally cannot take their eyes off the game. They need to see every play as it happens in order to record it precisely in the stat book or computer. Often, the official team scorer or statistician keeps track of certain statistics, while other statisticians keep track of the remaining statistics. For example, the official team scorer for a professional basketball team is responsible for tracking the field goals attempted and the field goals made, the three-point shots attempted and made, the free throws attempted and made, the number of personal fouls, and the number of time-outs taken. He or she may record other statistics, but if there is a discrepancy it is these stats for which he or she is responsible during the game. A team of statisticians who work the computers are responsible for taking down the number of rebounds, assists, steals, and so on. The most important aspect of the job is to remember that the statistician is doing more than compiling statistics; the statistician is recording the game, event by event.

Statisticians also work for television and radio stations and the sports information departments of colleges and universities. The jobs of these statisticians are nearly identical to that of the official team statistician for a professional team, in that they might record statistics in a manner similar to the one described above, but they might also be asked to do a lot of research and writing. Television stations often have a statistics and research staff responsible for collecting and verifying the statistics of any given sport. If the sport is fairly popular, they might assign someone to cover the events in that area, but if the sport is relatively young or not as popular, they might be asked to research information and statistics for that sport. The statistics and information are usually passed along to the sportscasters who are covering a game or event in that sport. Often, the statisticians are asked to write up notes for the sportscasters to use. For example, if the sportscasters are covering a baseball game, the statistician might come up with trivia or examples throughout the history of baseball when someone pitched no-hitters (a game where a pitcher does not allow an opposing team's batters to get a hit through nine innings or more of play) back-to-back.

Statisticians who work for private companies might be asked to keep statistics, field calls from sportswriters the day after a game about the stats for that game, or write up notes for one of their company's clients—notes regarding stats or trivia, for example.

Statisticians work both part time and full time, depending on the level of athletics in which they are involved, their degree of computer literacy and education, and whether they pursue freelance or full-time employment opportunities. The vast majority of individuals work part time, simply because they enjoy keeping stats for a team in a sport they love. Competition is incredibly fierce for full-time positions, whether for a sports information department at a college or university, a radio or television station or network sports show, or a private statistics company. Most statisticians advise students interested in entering the field to be persistent in asking for volunteer or part-time positions, to keep their schedules open in the event someone does call with a chance to score a game, and to be realistic about the chances of finding full-time work.

Books to Read

Albert, Jim. *Teaching Statistics Using Baseball.* Washington, D.C.: Mathematical Association of America, 2003.
Albert, Jim, Jay Bennett, and James J. Cochran. *Anthology of Statistics in Sports.* Philadelphia: Society for Industrial and Applied Mathematics, 2005.
Donnelly, Robert A., Jr. *The Complete Idiot's Guide to Statistics.* 2d ed. New York: Alpha, 2007.
Ross, Ken. *A Mathematician at the Ballpark: Odds and Probabilities for Baseball Fans.* New York: Plume Books, 2007.
Rumsey, Deborah. *Statistics for Dummies.* New York: For Dummies, 2003.

REQUIREMENTS

High School

Technically, there are no formal educational requirements for the job of sports statistician. Knowing how to manually score a game or event, and knowing as much as possible about the sport or sports for which you would like to keep statistics, are probably the only true requirements, but there are plenty of informal requirements that prospective sports statisticians should keep in mind.

First and foremost, although knowledge of manual scoring is essential, the future of sports statistics, like almost everything else, is tied to computers. The more you know about computers, from navigating your way around a keyboard to programming and troubleshooting, the better. Since most of the computer systems for the professional teams are privately owned, created expressly for the league or association, there isn't any way to study the programs used by professional teams while in high school or later. Becoming computer literate and having a working knowledge of common computer systems and programs, however, is the best way to ensure that, if necessary, you can pick up the intricacies of a new program after graduation.

Second, having a solid grasp of basic math skills is a necessity. In order to compute home run averages, you need to be able to figure averages. The formulas used to arrive at the different statistics are simple enough, but you must be good with math to figure them out yourself. On the job you will probably use a calculator or computer, but if the computer system goes out you need to be able to do the math yourself. Take as many math classes as possible while in high school to build a strong foundation.

Good writing and communication skills are also vital to the statistician; you may find yourself trying to explain a statistic to a sportscaster or writer, or you may be asked to write notes concerning relevant statistics or trivia, even a press release. If you can't communicate information quickly and intelligently, you might find yourself out of a job. For this reason, take English literature and writing courses to develop your language skills while in high school.

Postsecondary Training

Private companies that employ sports statisticians will most likely require candidates to have a bachelor's degree in statistics or in a related field, such as marketing, accounting, communications, or sports administration.

Other Requirements

To be a successful sports statistician, you need to be accurate, detail oriented, and thorough in your work. You should have good vision and be able to keep your concentration fully focused on the game at hand. Most importantly, you should enjoy athletics and competition. Many sports statisticians work part time for reasons as simple as a love of the game.

EXPLORING

The best way to gain experience in this field is to learn as much as possible about how a sport is played and how to score it, especially those sports that you enjoy most. High school and college students can easily accomplish this by participating in sports or volunteering to act as statistician for one of the teams. If neither of these options is available, then simply by avidly attending games and scoring the various aspects of the game, whatever they may be, you can begin to pick up the finer points of scoring. In some sports, however, there are rather complicated statistics to score, such as earned run averages in baseball.

There are books available for nearly every sport that explain, in detail, how to correctly score particular statistics, but there is a better, more expedient way. Look around you at the next high school baseball or basketball game. Chances are a seasoned veteran of statistics is no less than two yards away. During a break or, better yet, after the game, introduce yourself and ask that person how to score a game. Most statisticians learned how to score sports events in precisely this way—by asking the people who have been doing it for years.

Another good reason for getting to know the professional scorers in this way is that one day they might need someone to cover a game, or know of an opening for a part-time statistician.

EMPLOYERS

Approximately 19,000 statisticians are employed in the United States, but sports statisticians make up only a very small portion of this group. Sports statisticians work for professional athletic teams, television and radio stations and networks, private companies, and college and university sports programs.

STARTING OUT

Many statisticians find part-time jobs when they are high school students and continue these jobs through college. Others go on to score stats for various teams at their college or university. The sports information departments at colleges and universities are also good places to look for part-time work. You might be assigned to the public relations office, in which case you would learn the related tasks, such as fielding calls from the media, writing press releases, and researching statistics for a specific team. Or, you might be assigned to work directly with a team as a statistician. In either case, many statisticians continue to volunteer or work part time at stats jobs in order to maintain their scoring skills.

Television and radio stations are yet another way into the field of sports statistics. As mentioned, contacts are very helpful, but you can send your resume to the sports departments of various stations and channels, asking if they need another statistician. Be ready to volunteer if necessary or to work in the sometimes-humbling position of a gofer. One longtime statistician advises prospective statisticians to be ready to score any game, anytime, anywhere, because one never knows which contact will eventually lead to something bigger and better. This also means being prepared to sacrifice personal time to a last-minute request from a statistician to cover a game in an emergency when he or she can't be there.

Finally, there are three companies that work with sports statistics: Elias Sports Bureau, PA Sport, and STATS. These companies employ statisticians and researchers to help provide clients (television, radio, and cable stations; magazines and newspapers) with sports statistics and research on a daily basis. These companies often offer internships and part-time jobs and are definitely one avenue to pursue for full-time jobs.

ADVANCEMENT

Part-time jobs keeping statistics for high school and college and university athletic teams can often lead to stats jobs with other organizations, including radio and television stations and private organizations, such as Elias Sports Bureau, PA Sport, and STATS. While not much of a hierarchy exists in these companies (most employees are either statisticians and researchers or executives), it is possible to advance to executive-level positions within these companies. While some people may leave these jobs to take others, most stay in these jobs for many years.

Statisticians who build solid reputations, who know the ins and outs of a particular sport, and who have excellent communication and math skills can often advance in the field to work for large radio and television networks.

EARNINGS

On the whole, competition will be keen for full-time jobs that offer competitive salaries in sports statistics. It is important to realize that many statisticians must work full-time jobs, often in totally unrelated fields, in order to support themselves. Only their love of the sport and statistics itself—and not the financial rewards of the jobs—keeps them involved with sports statistics.

Even for part-timers, much depends on the level of athletics in which the statistician is involved. For example, a statistician working freelance for a radio station covering the Memphis Grizzlies (an expansion professional basketball team) might receive $35 per game, whereas a statistician working freelance for one of the large television networks, such as Fox, might receive anywhere from $400 to $500 per game.

On the other hand, statisticians who work full time for radio and television, or for companies like Elias Sports Bureau, receive salaries commensurate with jobs in other fields. An individual working with one of these companies for between one year and five years might earn $25,000 to $35,000 a year. If that person stayed with the company for another five to 10 years, he or she might earn between $35,000 and $50,000 a year. Statisticians who work for a company for many years can earn anywhere between $75,000 and $100,000 a year. Again, competition for these positions is extremely fierce.

In comparison to statisticians who work in the more traditional fields of statistical analysis, both in government and nongovernment jobs, sports statisticians with full-time positions have the opportunity to earn considerably higher salaries, although this may not always be the case. According to the U.S. Department of Labor, the median annual salary for statisticians was $65,720 in 2006. Salaries ranged from less than $37,010 to more than $108,630.

WORK ENVIRONMENT

Statisticians routinely work in the same conditions as do others in professions related to sports coverage, such as sportscasters, sportswriters, and sports agents. That is, they may spend time outdoors, in pleasant and inclement weather, but they also spend a lot of time indoors, in the media and statistics areas of sports stadiums and arenas, and in their own offices.

Statisticians also work odd hours, including weekends and holidays. In short, whenever there is a sports event scheduled that requires scorekeeping and statistics, one or more statisticians will be covering it. This can wreak havoc with the more nostalgic of holidays, such as Christmas and the Fourth of July; some football and many basketball games are scheduled on Christmas Eve and Christmas Day, while there are countless professional baseball games played on Independence Day.

OUTLOOK

As the impact of cable and satellite television enhances the marketability of the top five sports (football, baseball, basketball, hockey, and soccer), it will also bring into viewers' living rooms many sports not previously carried by the major networks. All of this increased sports coverage, plus developing technologies and markets on the Internet, will only increase the demand for sports statistics and the individuals who record and catalog them. More importantly, perhaps, is the effect this new technology will have on those seeking jobs in sports statistics, as computer skills will become just as valuable to those interested in a career in sports statistics as in-depth knowledge of a sport. Those individuals who do have computer skills will be all the more marketable in the years to come. People already in the field will probably want to develop some degree of computer literacy.

On another note, even as the field develops, those currently with full-time positions in sports statistics aren't likely to leave those jobs. Attrition rates due to retirement and advancement, combined with the addition of some new positions, should keep this field developing about as fast as the average for all other occupations.

FOR MORE INFORMATION

For information on careers in statistics or schools that offer degrees in statistics, contact
American Statistical Association
732 North Washington Street
Alexandria, VA 22314-1943
Tel: 888-231-3473
Email: asainfo@amstat.org
http://www.amstat.org

The following companies employ statisticians and researchers. Visit their Web sites for more information.
Elias Sports Bureau
http://www.esb.com

PA Sport
http://www.sportsticker.com

STATS
http://www.stats.com

Statisticians

OVERVIEW

Statisticians use mathematical theories to collect and interpret information. This information is used to help various agencies, industries, and researchers determine the best ways to produce results in their work. There are approximately 19,000 statisticians in the United States, employed in a wide variety of work fields, including government, industry, and scientific research.

HISTORY

One of the first known uses of statistical technique was in England in the mid-1800s, when a disastrous epidemic of cholera broke out in a section of London. A local physician named John Snow decided to conduct a survey to determine what sections of the city were affected by the disease. He then constructed a map showing how the infection was distributed and interviewed people who had survived the illness about their living habits. He discovered that everyone who had contracted the illness had drawn water from a certain pump in the area. Once the pump was sealed, the cholera epidemic subsided. Because of Snow's research, medical professionals were able to learn that cholera was transmitted through an infected water supply. His use of statistical methods therefore uncovered a fact that has since saved countless lives.

In its simplest form, statistics is a science that organizes many facts into a systematized picture of data. Modern statistics is based on the theory of probability, and the work of statisticians has been greatly enhanced by the invention of computers.

The need for statisticians has grown by leaps and bounds in modern times. Since 1945, the number of universities with programs

Mathematical statisticians review data for a community's nutrition mapping project. *(Stephen Ausmus, Agricultural Research Service, U.S. Department of Agriculture)*

leading to graduate degrees in statistics has jumped from a half-dozen to more than 130. One reason for the increased demand is that statistical methods have many important uses. For example, methods similar to those used to study waves from distant galaxies can also be used to analyze blood hormone levels, track financial market fluctuations, and find concentrations of atmospheric pollutants. Experts predict that the demand for such useful statistical methodology will continue to grow.

Statistics are now used in all areas of science as well as in industry and business. Government officials are especially dependent on statistics—from politicians to education officials to traffic controllers.

THE JOB

Statisticians use their knowledge of mathematics and statistical theory to collect and interpret information. They determine whether data are reliable and useful and search for facts that will help solve scientific questions.

Most statisticians work in one of three kinds of jobs: they may teach and do research at a large university, they may work for a government agency (such as the U.S. Census Bureau), or they may work in a business or industry. A few statisticians work in private consulting agencies and sell their services to industrial or government organizations. Other statisticians work in well-known public opinion research organizations. Their studies help us understand what groups of people think about major issues of the day or products on the market.

There are two major areas of statistics: mathematical statistics and applied statistics. *Mathematical statisticians* are primarily theoreticians. They develop and test new statistical methods and theories and devise new ways in which these methods can be applied. They also work on improving existing methods and formulas.

Applied statisticians apply existing theories or known formulas to make new predictions or discoveries. They may forecast population growth or economic conditions, estimate crop yield, predict and evaluate the result of a marketing program, or help engineers and scientists determine the best design for a jet airline.

In some cases, statisticians actually go out and gather the data to be analyzed. Usually, however, they receive data from individuals trained especially in research-gathering techniques. In the U.S. Census Bureau, for example, statisticians work with material that has been compiled by thousands of census takers. Once the census takers have gathered the data, they turn the information over to statisticians for organization, analysis, and conclusions or recommendations.

Statisticians are employed in many sectors of society. One of the largest employers of statisticians is the government, because many government operations depend on detailed estimates of activities. Government data on consumer prices, population trends, and employment patterns, for example, can affect public policy and social programs.

Statistical models and methods are also necessary for all types of scientific research. For example, a geoscientist estimating earthquake risks or ecologists measuring water quality both use statistical methods to determine the validity of their results. In business and industry, statistical theories are used to figure out how to streamline operations, optimize resources, and, as a result, generate higher profits. For instance, statisticians may predict demand for a product, check the quality of manufactured items, or manage investments.

The insurance industry also uses statisticians to calculate fair and competitive insurance rates and to forecast the risk of underwriting activities. Ben Lamb is a statistician for Grain Dealers Mutual Insurance in Indianapolis. When asked to sum up his job, he says, "I get data into the computers, get data back out, and send out reports." The data he puts into the computer include the specific details of policies signed, insurance premiums paid, and insurance claims made.

Once this information is in the computer, it is plugged into statistical formulas and used to generate reports. "We make detailed reports to our own management," Lamb says. "We also file required reports with the National Insurance Services Office." This national office compiles insurance data from all over the nation and uses the information to generate reports that are then sent to the insurance commissioners of the various states.

Lamb says that his office collects data and runs reports at the end of every workday, as well as once a month. "We have a daily flow of work," he says. "The information comes in during the day, and we process it to get it ready for that night." Processing the information may mean editing to ensure that it is correct, or "coding" it, that is, assigning short number or letter codes to the information so that the computer can understand and manipulate the data.

REQUIREMENTS

High School
If you are interested in the field of statistics, you should take classes that will prepare you for college, since you will need at least a bachelor's degree to qualify for jobs. Focus on mathematics (including statistics classes), computers, and science classes, but don't neglect other college preparatory courses such as English and a foreign language.

Postsecondary Training
Statisticians usually graduate from college with strong mathematics and computer backgrounds. Bachelor's degrees in statistics, mathematics, or biostatistics are available at approximately 230 colleges and universities in the United States. Classes include differential and integral calculus, mathematical modeling, statistical methods, and probability. Other students major in the field they hope to work in, such as chemistry, agriculture, or psychology.

Although a bachelor's degree is the minimum needed to become a statistician, your chances for success are better if you earn an advanced degree. Many positions are open only to those with a master's or doctorate. Approximately 140 universities offer a master's degree program in statistics, and about 90 have doctorate programs in statistics.

Other Requirements
Prospective statisticians should be able to think in terms of mathematical concepts. According to Ben Lamb, however, the ability to

think logically is even more important for a good statistician. "Math skills are not as important as logic," he says. "You have to be able to use logic in the processing of statistics."

Statisticians should also have a strong curiosity that will prompt them to explore any given subject. Finally, a good statistician should be detail oriented and able to handle stress well. "You have to be very attentive to details, but you can't be too much of a perfection-ist," Lamb says, "because there are too many things that can go wrong when you're dealing with a computer system. You have to be able to deal with problems if there is something wrong with the system, because it does happen."

EXPLORING

While in high school, ask your math teachers to give you some simple statistical problems, perhaps related to grades or student government. This will allow you to practice the kinds of techniques that statisticians use. If you want to explore the profession further, you might visit a local insurance agency, the local office of the Internal Revenue Service, or a nearby college and talk to people who use statistical methods.

College students can frequently obtain jobs as student assistants in the offices of faculty members who are engaged in some kind of research. Although these jobs may seem to carry little responsibility, undergraduate students can gain some insight into and practice in research methods.

EMPLOYERS

There are approximately 19,000 statisticians employed in the United States. The federal government, such as the Departments of Commerce, Health and Human Services, and Agriculture, as well as the Census Bureau, employs about 20 percent of these workers. Another 20 percent work for state and local governments. Of the remaining statisticians, most work in private industry. Private-industry employers include insurance companies, research and testing services, management and public relations firms, computer and data processing firms, manufacturing companies, and the financial services sector. Statisticians also work in colleges and universities in teaching and research positions.

Jobs for statisticians can be found throughout the United States but are concentrated most heavily in large metropolitan areas such as New York, Chicago, Los Angeles, and Washington, D.C.

STARTING OUT

Most new graduates find positions through their college career services offices. "We get most of our applicants through placement offices and agencies," Ben Lamb says. "We have very few walk-ins."

For those students who are particularly interested in working for a government agency, jobs are listed with the Office of Personnel Management. Some government jobs may be obtained only after the successful passing of a civil service examination. College-level teaching is normally only open to candidates with doctorates. College teaching jobs are usually obtained by making a direct application to the dean of the school or college in which the statistics department is located.

ADVANCEMENT

A statistician with a bachelor's degree will probably begin in a position that involves primarily routine or clerical work, such as the job of junior statistician. Advancement may be seen more in terms of gradually increased pay rather than greater job responsibilities. After having acquired experience on the job and value to the employer, the statistician may be promoted to chief statistician, director of research, or, in teaching positions, full professor. Advancement can take many years, and it usually requires returning to graduate school or a special technical school to achieve a higher degree or more skills. Statisticians who advance most rapidly to positions of responsibility are usually those with advanced degrees.

EARNINGS

The U.S. Department of Labor reports that the median annual salary for all statisticians was $65,720 in 2006; the highest paid group earned over $108,630, while the lowest paid group earned less than $37,010. The National Association of Colleges and Employers reports that starting-salary offers for mathematics and statistics graduates averaged $43,448 a year in 2005. Statisticians employed by the federal government earned mean annual salaries of $85,460 in 2006. Earnings for statisticians in private industry are generally somewhat higher.

Salaries for statisticians working in colleges and universities differ, depending on their position and their amount of experience. According to the *2006–2007 Salary Report of Academic Statisticians* from the American Statistical Association, the median salary for assistant professors working in research institutions ranged from $67,500 to $70,400 based on their amount of experience. Full professors might expect to earn anywhere from $93,550 to $122,750. In liberal arts institutions, assistant professors earned a median salary of $59,950. Full professors earned between $81,592 and $106,850 a year based on their amount of experience. Most statisticians receive a benefits package from their employer that typically includes paid sick and vacation time, health insurance, and some sort of retirement plan.

WORK ENVIRONMENT

Ben Lamb works Monday through Friday, from 8:00 A.M. to 4:15 P.M. Other statisticians in his department, however, work different hours. "We have flex time, because we have to have someone here at all times to process the data and back up the system."

While at work, Lamb spends the majority of his time working on a computer. Because this field of work is so heavily computerized, most statisticians' jobs will include a substantial amount of time on a computer.

Most statisticians work under pleasant circumstances, with regular work hours. In private industry or government, statisticians work in an office setting. Some may travel to collaborate on larger research projects. In academia, statisticians often split their time between teaching and conducting research.

OUTLOOK

Employment for statisticians is expected to grow more slowly than the average for all occupations through 2014, according to the U.S. Department of Labor. Even so, trained statisticians with advanced degrees or specialized training in computer science, engineering, or finance will have good job opportunities.

The federal government will continue to need statisticians for various agencies (for example, in Social Security, environmental protection, and demography), though competition is predicted to be high. Private industry will continue to need statisticians, especially in the pharmaceutical and automobile industries.

Opportunities for statisticians increase with level of education. Graduates with a bachelor's degree in mathematics and computer science are most likely to find jobs in applied statistics in private industry or government. With proper certification, they may teach statistics in high schools. In other cases, job seekers with bachelor's degrees may take entry-level jobs that do not have the formal job title of statistician. However, their work will involve much of the same processes, such as analyzing and interpreting data in economics, engineering, or biological science.

Statisticians with a master's degree and knowledge of computer science should find openings in private industry in statistical computing and in research. These candidates can also teach in junior colleges and small four-year colleges. The employment outlook is best for those with doctorates in statistics. These individuals are eagerly sought by large corporations as consultants, and they are also in demand by colleges and universities.

FOR MORE INFORMATION

For information on careers in statistics or schools that offer degrees in statistics, contact
American Statistical Association
732 North Washington Street
Alexandria, VA 22314-1943
Tel: 888-231-3473
Email: asainfo@amstat.org
http://www.amstat.org

For information on educational and employment opportunities for women in statistics and related fields, contact
Association for Women in Mathematics
11240 Waples Mill Road, Suite 200
Fairfax, VA 22030-6078
Tel: 703-934-0163
Email: awm@awm-math.org
http://www.awm-math.org

For information on student competitions, contact
Mathematical Association of America
1529 18th Street, NW
Washington, DC 20036-1358
Tel: 800-741-9415
http://www.maa.org

For a brochure on careers in applied mathematics, contact
Society for Industrial and Applied Mathematics
3600 Market Street, 6th Floor
Philadelphia, PA 19104-2688

Tel: 215-382-9800
http://www.siam.org

For information on schools and career opportunities in statistics in Canada, contact
Statistical Society of Canada
577 King Edward Avenue
Ottawa, ON K1N 6N5 Canada
Tel: 613-562-5320
Email: info@ssc.ca
http://www.ssc.ca

Surveyors

OVERVIEW

Surveyors mark exact measurements and locations of elevations, points, lines, and contours on or near the earth's surface. They measure distances between points to determine property boundaries and to provide data for mapmaking, construction projects, and other engineering purposes. There are approximately 131,000 surveyors, cartographers, photogrammetrists, and surveying technicians employed in the United States. Of those, about 56,000 are surveyors and about 11,000 are cartographers and photogrammetrists.

HISTORY

As the United States expanded from the Atlantic to the Pacific, people moved over the mountains and plains into the uncharted regions of the West. They found it necessary to chart their routes and to mark property lines and borderlines by surveying and filing claims.

The need for accurate geographical measurements and precise records of those measurements has increased over the years. Surveying measurements are needed to determine the location of a trail, highway, or road; the site of a log cabin, frame house, or skyscraper; the right-of-way for water pipes, drainage ditches, and telephone lines; and for the charting of unexplored regions, bodies of water, land, and underground mines.

As a result, the demand for professional surveyors has grown and become more complex. New computerized systems are now used to map, store, and retrieve geographical data more accurately and efficiently. This new technology has not only improved the process

QUICK FACTS

School Subjects
Geography
Mathematics

Personal Skills
Communication/ideas
Technical/scientific

Work Environment
Primarily outdoors
Primarily multiple locations

Minimum Education Level
Some postsecondary training

Salary Range
$26,690 to $48,290 to $79,910+

Certification or Licensing
Required

Outlook
About as fast as the average

DOT
018

GOE
02.08.01

NOC
2154

O*NET-SOC
17-1022.00

of surveying but extended its reach as well. Surveyors can now make detailed maps of ocean floors and the moon's surface.

THE JOB

On proposed construction projects, such as highways, airstrips, and housing developments, it is the surveyor's responsibility to make necessary measurements through an accurate and detailed survey of the area. The surveyor usually works with a field party consisting of several people. Instrument assistants, called *surveying and mapping technicians*, handle a variety of surveying instruments including the theodolite, transit, level, surveyor's chain, rod, and other electronic equipment. In the course of the survey, it is important that all readings be recorded accurately and field notes maintained so that the survey can be checked for accuracy.

Surveyors may specialize in one or more particular types of surveying.

Land surveyors establish township, property, and other tract-of-land boundary lines. Using maps, notes, or actual land title deeds, they survey the land, checking for the accuracy of existing records. This information is used to prepare legal documents such as deeds and leases. *Land surveying managers* coordinate the work of surveyors, their parties, and legal, engineering, architectural, and other staff involved in a project. In addition, these managers develop policy, prepare budgets, certify work upon completion, and handle numerous other administrative duties.

Highway surveyors establish grades, lines, and other points of reference for highway construction projects. This survey information is essential to the work of the numerous engineers and the construction crews who build the new highway.

Geodetic surveyors measure large masses of land, sea, and space that must take into account the curvature of the earth and its geophysical characteristics. Their work is helpful in establishing points of reference for smaller land surveys, determining national boundaries, and preparing maps. Geodetic computers calculate latitude, longitude, angles, areas, and other information needed for mapmaking. They work from field notes made by an engineering survey party and also use reference tables and a calculating machine or computer.

Marine surveyors measure harbors, rivers, and other bodies of water. They determine the depth of the water through measuring sound waves in relation to nearby landmasses. Their work is essential for planning and constructing navigation projects, such as

Surveyors must be able to work with numbers and perform mathematical computations accurately and quickly. *(Bob Daemmrich, The Image Works)*

breakwaters, dams, piers, marinas, and bridges, and for preparing nautical charts and maps.

Mine surveyors make surface and underground surveys, preparing maps of mines and mining operations. Such maps are helpful in examining underground passages within the levels of a mine and assessing the volume and location of raw material available.

Geophysical prospecting surveyors locate and mark sites considered likely to contain petroleum deposits. *Oil well directional surveyors* use sonic, electronic, and nuclear measuring instruments to gauge the presence and amount of oil- and gas-bearing reservoirs. *Pipeline surveyors* determine rights-of-way for oil construction projects, providing information essential to the preparation for and laying of the lines.

Photogrammetric engineers determine the contour of an area to show elevations and depressions and indicate such features as mountains, lakes, rivers, forests, roads, farms, buildings, and other landmarks. Aerial, land, and water photographs are taken with special equipment able to capture images of very large areas. From these pictures, accurate measurements of the terrain and surface features can be made. These surveys are helpful in construction projects and in the preparation of topographical maps. Photogrammetry is particularly helpful in charting areas that are inaccessible or difficult to travel.

REQUIREMENTS

High School
Does this work interest you? If so, you should prepare for it by taking plenty of math and science courses in high school. Take algebra, geometry, and trigonometry to become comfortable making different calculations. Earth science, chemistry, and physics classes should also be helpful. Geography will help you learn about different locations, their characteristics, and cartography. Benefits from taking mechanical drawing and other drafting classes include an increased ability to visualize abstractions, exposure to detailed work, and an understanding of perspectives. Taking computer science classes will prepare you for working with technical surveying equipment.

Postsecondary Training
Depending on state requirements, you will need some postsecondary education. The quickest route is by earning a bachelor's degree in surveying or engineering combined with on-the-job training. Other entry options include obtaining more job experience combined with a one- to three-year program in surveying and surveying technology offered by community colleges, technical institutes, and vocational schools.

Certification or Licensing

All 50 states require that surveyors making property and boundary surveys be licensed or registered. The requirements for licensure vary, but most require a degree in surveying or a related field, a certain number of years of experience, and passing of examinations in land surveying. Generally, the higher the degree obtained, the less experience required. Those with bachelor's degrees may need only two to four years of on-the-job experience, while those with a lesser degree may need up to 12 years of prior experience to obtain a license. Information on specific requirements can be obtained by contacting the licensure department of the state in which you plan to work. If you are seeking employment in the federal government, you must take a civil service examination and meet the educational, experience, and other specified requirements for the position.

Other Requirements

The ability to work with numbers and perform mathematical computations accurately and quickly is very important. Other helpful qualities are the ability to visualize and understand objects in two and three dimensions (spatial relationships) and the ability to discriminate between and compare shapes, sizes, lines, shadings, and other forms (form perception).

Surveyors walk a great deal and carry equipment over all types of terrain so endurance and coordination are important physical assets. In addition, surveyors direct and supervise the work of their team, so you should be good at working with other people and demonstrate leadership abilities.

EXPLORING

While you are in high school, begin to familiarize yourself with terms, projects, and tools used in this profession by reading books and magazines on the topic. One magazine that is available online is *Professional Surveyor Magazine* at http://www.profsurv.com. Among the best opportunities for experience is a summer job with a construction outfit or company that requires survey work. Even if the job does not involve direct contact with survey crews, it will offer an opportunity to observe surveyors and talk with them about their work.

Some colleges have work-study programs that offer on-the-job experience. These opportunities, like summer or part-time jobs, provide helpful contacts in the field that may lead to future full-time employment. If your college does not offer a work-study program and you can't find a paying summer job, consider volunteering at an appropriate government agency. The U.S. Geological Survey and the Bureau of Land Management usually have volunteer opportunities in select areas.

EMPLOYERS

According to the U.S. Department of Labor, almost two-thirds of surveying workers in the United States are employed in engineering, architectural, and surveying firms. Federal, state, and local government agencies are the next largest employers of surveying workers, and the majority of the remaining surveyors work for construction firms, oil and gas extraction companies, and public utilities. Only a small number of surveyors are self-employed.

STARTING OUT

Apprentices with a high school education can enter the field as equipment operators or surveying assistants. Those who have postsecondary education can enter the field more easily, beginning as surveying and mapping technicians.

College graduates can learn about job openings through their schools' career services offices or through potential employers that may visit their campus. Many cities have employment agencies that specialize in seeking out workers for positions in surveying and related fields. Check your local newspaper or telephone book to see if such recruiting firms exist in your area.

ADVANCEMENT

With experience, workers advance through the leadership ranks within a surveying team. Workers begin as assistants and then can move into positions such as senior technician, party chief, and, finally, licensed surveyor. Because surveying work is closely related to other fields, surveyors can move into electrical, mechanical, or chemical engineering or specialize in drafting.

EARNINGS

In 2006, surveyors earned a median annual salary of $48,290, according to the U.S. Department of Labor. The middle 50 percent earned between $35,720 and $63,990 a year. The lowest paid 10 percent earned less than $26,690, and the highest paid 10 percent earned more than $79,910 a year. In general, the federal government paid the highest mean wages to its surveyors, $72,180 a year in 2006.

Most positions with the federal, state, and local governments and with private firms provide life and medical insurance, pension, vacation, and holiday benefits.

WORK ENVIRONMENT

Surveyors work 40-hour weeks except when overtime is necessary to meet a project deadline. The peak work period is during the summer months when weather conditions are most favorable. However, it is not uncommon for the surveyor to be exposed to adverse weather conditions.

Some survey projects may involve hazardous conditions, depending on the region and climate as well as the plant and animal life. Survey crews may encounter snakes, poison ivy, and other hazardous plant and animal life, and may suffer heat exhaustion, sunburn, and frostbite while in the field. Survey projects, particularly those near construction projects or busy highways, may impose dangers of injury from heavy traffic, flying objects, and other accidental hazards. Unless the surveyor is employed only for office assignments, the work location most likely will change from survey to survey. Some assignments may require the surveyor to be away from home for periods of time.

OUTLOOK

The U.S. Department of Labor predicts that the employment of surveyors will grow about as fast as the average for all occupations through 2014. The outlook is best for surveyors who have college degrees and advanced field experience. Despite slower growth, the widespread use of technology, such as the Global Positioning System and geographic information systems, will provide jobs to surveyors with strong technical and computer skills.

Growth in urban and suburban areas (with the need for new streets, homes, shopping centers, schools, gas and water lines) will provide employment opportunities. State and federal highway improvement programs and local urban redevelopment programs also will provide jobs for surveyors. The expansion of industrial and business firms and the relocation of some firms to large undeveloped tracts will also create job openings. However, construction projects are closely tied to the state of the economy, so employment may fluctuate from year to year.

FOR MORE INFORMATION

For information on state affiliates and colleges and universities offering land surveying programs, contact
American Congress on Surveying and Mapping
Six Montgomery Village Avenue, Suite 403
Gaithersburg, MD 20879-3546
Tel: 240-632-9716
http://www.acsm.net

For information on awards and recommended books to read, contact or check out the following organizations' Web sites:
American Association for Geodetic Surveying
Six Montgomery Village Avenue, Suite 403
Gaithersburg, MD 20879-3546
Tel: 240-632-9716
Email: aagsmo@acsm.net
http://www.aagsmo.org

National Society of Professional Surveyors
Six Montgomery Village Avenue, Suite 403
Gaithersburg, MD 20879-3557
Tel: 240-632-9716
http://www.nspsmo.org

For information on photogrammetry and careers in the field, contact
American Society for Photogrammetry and Remote Sensing
5410 Grosvenor Lane, Suite 210
Bethesda, MD 20814-2160
Tel: 301-493-0290
Email: asprs@asprs.org
http://www.asprs.org

For information on volunteer opportunities with the federal government, contact the following organizations:
Bureau of Land Management
Office of Public Affairs
1849 C Street, Room 406-LS
Washington, DC 20240-0001
Tel: 202-452-5125
http://www.blm.gov

U.S. Geological Survey
12201 Sunrise Valley Drive
Reston, VA 20192-0002
Tel: 703-648-4000
http://www.usgs.gov

Tax Preparers

OVERVIEW

Tax preparers prepare income tax returns for individuals and small businesses for a fee, for either quarterly or yearly filings. They help to establish and maintain business records to expedite tax preparations and may advise clients on how to save money on their tax payments. There are approximately 86,000 tax preparers employed in the United States.

HISTORY

President Franklin D. Roosevelt once said, "Taxes are the dues that we pay for the privileges of membership in an organized society." Although most people grumble about paying income taxes and filling out tax forms, everyone carries a share of the burden, and it is still possible to keep a sense of humor about income taxes. As Benjamin Franklin succinctly said, "In this world nothing can be said to be certain, except death and taxes."

While the personal income tax may be the most familiar type of taxation, it is actually a relatively recent method of raising revenue. To raise funds for the Napoleonic Wars between 1799 and 1816, Britain became the first nation to collect income taxes, but a permanent income tax was not established there until 1874. In the same manner, the United States first initiated a temporary income tax during the Civil War. It wasn't until 1913, however, with the adoption of the 16th Amendment to the Constitution, that a tax on personal income became the law of the nation. In addition to the federal income tax, many states and cities have adopted income tax laws. Income taxes are an example of a "progressive tax," one that charges higher percentages of income as people earn more money.

Technology has now made it possible to file taxes electronically. Electronic tax filing is a method by which a tax return is converted to computer-readable form and sent via modem to the Internal Revenue Service. Electronically filed tax returns are more accurate than paper filed returns because of the extensive checking performed by the electronic filing software. Detecting and correcting errors early also allows the tax return to flow smoothly through the IRS, speeding up the refund process. New computer software is also available that assists individuals with preparing and filing their own taxes.

THE JOB

Tax preparers help individuals and small businesses keep the proper records to determine their legally required tax and file the proper forms. They must be well acquainted with federal, state, and local tax laws and use their knowledge and skills to help taxpayers take the maximum number of legally allowable deductions.

The first step in preparing tax forms is to collect all the data and documents that are needed to calculate the client's tax liability. The client has to submit documents such as tax returns from previous years, wage and income statements, records of other sources of income, statements of interest and dividends earned, records of expenses, property tax records, and so on. The tax preparer then interviews the client to obtain further information that may have a bearing on the amount of tax owed. If the client is an individual taxpayer, the tax preparer will ask about any important investments, extra expenses that may be deductible, contributions to charity, and insurance payments; events such as marriage, childbirth, and new employment are also important considerations. If the client is a business, the tax preparer may ask about capital gains and losses, taxes already paid, payroll expenses, miscellaneous business expenses, and tax credits.

Once the tax preparer has a complete picture of the client's income and expenses, the proper tax forms and schedules needed to file the tax return can be determined. While some taxpayers have very complex finances that take a long time to document and calculate, others have typical, straightforward returns that take less time. Often the tax preparer can calculate the amount a taxpayer owes, fill out the proper forms, and prepare the complete return in a single interview. When the tax return is more complicated, the tax preparer may have to collect all the data during the interview and perform the calculations later. If a client's taxes are unusual or very complex, the tax preparer may have to consult tax law handbooks and bulletins.

Computers are the main tools used to figure and prepare tax returns. The tax preparer inputs the data onto a spreadsheet, and the computer calculates and prints out the tax form. Computer software can be very versatile and may even print up data summary sheets that can serve as checklists and references for the next tax filing.

Tax preparers often have another tax expert or preparer check their work, especially if they work for a tax service firm. The second tax preparer will check to make sure the allowances and deductions taken were proper and that no others were overlooked. They also make certain that the tax laws are interpreted properly and that calculations are correct. It is very important that a tax preparer's work is accurate and error free, and clients are given a guarantee covering additional taxes or fines if the preparer's work is found to be incorrect. Tax preparers are required by law to sign every return they complete for a client and provide their Social Security number or federal identification number. They must also provide the client with a copy of the tax return and keep a copy in their own files.

REQUIREMENTS

High School

Although there are no specific postsecondary educational requirements for tax preparers, you should certainly get your high school diploma. While you are in high school there are a number of classes you can take that will help prepare you for this type of work. You should take mathematics classes. Accounting, bookkeeping, and business classes will also give you a feel for working with numbers and show you the importance of accurate work. In addition, take computer classes. You will need to be comfortable using computers, since much tax work is done using this tool. Finally, take English classes. English classes will help you work on your research, writing, and speaking skills—important communication skills to have when you work with clients.

Postsecondary Training

Once you have completed high school, you may be able to find a job as a tax preparer at a large tax-preparation firm. These firms, such as H&R Block, typically require their tax preparers to complete a training program in tax preparation. If you would like to pursue a college education, many universities offer individual courses and complete majors in the area of taxation. Another route is to earn a bachelor's degree or master's degree in business administration with a minor or concentration in taxation. A few universities offer master's degrees in taxation.

In addition to formal education, tax preparers must continue their professional education. Both federal and state tax laws are revised every year, and the tax preparer is obligated to understand these new laws thoroughly by January 1 of each year. Major tax reform legislation can increase this amount of study even further. One federal reform tax bill can take up thousands of pages, and this can mean up to 60 hours of extra study in a single month to fully understand all the intricacies and implications of the new laws. To help tax preparers keep up with new developments, the National Association of Tax Professionals offers more than 200 workshops every year. Tax service firms also offer classes explaining tax preparation to both professionals and individual taxpayers.

Certification or Licensing

Licensing requirements for tax preparers vary by state, and you should be sure to find out what requirements there are in the state where you wish to practice. Since 2002, for example, tax preparers in California have been required to register with the California Tax Education Council, a nonprofit corporation established by the California State Legislature to oversee tax preparation. Tax preparers who apply for registration in that state must be at least 18 years old. In addition, they need to have 60 hours of formal, approved instruction in basic income tax law, theory, and practice, or two years of professional experience in preparing personal income tax returns.

The Internal Revenue Service (IRS) offers an examination for tax preparers. Those who complete the test successfully are called enrolled agents and are entitled to legally represent any taxpayer in any type of audit before the IRS or state tax boards. (Those with five years' experience working for the IRS as an auditor or in a higher position can become enrolled agents without taking the exam.) The four-part test is offered annually and takes two days to complete. There are no education or experience requirements for taking the examination, but the questions are roughly equivalent to those asked in a college course. Study materials and applications may be obtained from local IRS offices. The IRS does not oversee seasonal tax preparers, but local IRS offices may monitor some commercial tax offices.

The Institute of Tax Consultants offers an annual open book exam to obtain the title of certified tax preparer. Certification also requires 30 hours of continuing education each year.

The Accreditation Council for Accountancy and Taxation confers the accredited tax preparer and accredited tax advisor designations on professionals who meet work experience and other requirements. Contact the council for more information.

Other Requirements

Tax preparers should have an aptitude for math and an eye for detail. They should have strong organizational skills and the patience to sift through documents and financial statements. The ability to communicate effectively with clients is also important to be able to explain complex tax procedures and to make customers feel confident and comfortable. Tax preparers also need to work well under the stress and pressure of deadlines. They must also be honest, discreet, and trustworthy in dealing with the financial and business affairs of their clients.

EXPLORING

If a career in tax preparation sounds interesting, you should first gain some experience by completing income tax returns for yourself and for your family and friends. These returns should be double-checked by the actual taxpayers who will be liable for any fees and extra taxes if the return is prepared incorrectly. You can also look for internships or part-time jobs in tax service offices and tax preparation firms. Many of these firms operate nationwide, and extra office help might be needed as tax deadlines approach and work becomes hectic. The IRS also trains people to answer tax questions for its 800-number telephone advisory service; they are employed annually during early spring.

Try also to familiarize yourself with the tax preparation software available on the Internet and use Web sites to keep abreast of changing laws, regulations, and developments in the industry. The National Association of Tax Professionals offers sample articles from its publications, *TAXPRO Quarterly* and *TAXPRO Monthly*, online. (See end of article for contact information.)

EMPLOYERS

Approximately 86,000 tax preparers are employed in the United States. Tax preparers may work for tax service firms that conduct most of their business during tax season. Other tax preparers may be self-employed and work full or part time.

STARTING OUT

Because tax work is very seasonal, most tax firms begin hiring tax preparers in December for the upcoming tax season. Some tax service firms will hire tax preparers from among the graduates of their own training courses. Private and state employment agencies may also have information and job listings, as will classified newspaper ads. You should also consult your school guidance offices to establish contacts in the field.

There are a large number of Internet sites for this industry, many of which offer job postings. Many large tax preparation firms, such as H&R Block, also have their own Web pages.

ADVANCEMENT

Some tax preparers may wish to continue their academic education and work toward becoming certified public accountants. Others may want to specialize in certain areas of taxation, such as real estate, corporate, or nonprofit work. Tax preparers who specialize in certain fields are able to charge higher fees for their services.

Establishing a private consulting business is also an option. Potential proprietors should consult with other self-employed practitioners to gain advice on how to start a private practice. Several Internet sites also give valuable advice on establishing a tax business.

EARNINGS

According to the U.S. Department of Labor, the median annual income for tax preparers was approximately $27,360 in 2006. Salaries ranged from less than $16,080 to more than $56,640 annually. Incomes can vary widely from these figures, however, due to a number of factors. One reason is that tax preparers generally charge a fee per tax return, which may range from $30 to $1,500 or more, depending on the complexity of the return and the preparation time required. Therefore, the number of clients a preparer has, as well as the difficulty of the returns, can affect the preparer's income. Another factor affecting income is the amount of education a tax preparer has. Seasonal or part-time employees, typically those with less education, usually earn minimum wage plus commission. Enrolled agents, certified public accountants, and other professional preparers, typically those with college degrees or more, usually charge more. Finally, it is important to realize that fees vary widely in different parts of the country. Tax preparers in large cities and in the western United States generally charge more, as do those who offer year-round financial advice and services.

WORK ENVIRONMENT

Tax preparers generally work in office settings that may be located in neighborhood business districts, shopping malls, or other high-traffic areas. Employees of tax service firms may work at storefront desks or in cubicles during the three months preceding the April 15 tax-filing deadline. In addition, many tax preparers work at home to earn extra money while they hold a full-time job.

The hours and schedules that tax preparers work vary greatly, depending on the time of year and the manner in which workers are employed. Because of the changes in tax laws that occur every year, tax preparers often advise their clients throughout the year about possible ways to reduce their tax obligations. The first quarter of the year is the busiest time, and even part-time tax preparers may find themselves working very long hours. Workweeks can range from as little as 12 hours to 40 or 50 or more, as tax preparers work late into the evening and on weekends. Tax service firms are usually open seven days a week and 12 hours a day during the first three months of the year. The work is demanding, requiring heavy concentration and long hours sitting at a desk and working on a computer.

OUTLOOK

The U.S. Department of Labor predicts that employment for tax preparers will grow about as fast as the average for all occupations through 2014. According to the IRS, over 50 percent of U.S. taxpayers used paid preparers to file their returns for the 2005 tax year, and because tax laws are constantly changing and growing more complex, demand for tax professionals will remain high. Much of this demand, however, is expected to be met by the tax preparers already working because computers are increasingly expediting the process of tabulating and storing data. Recent surveys of employers in large metropolitan areas have found an adequate supply of tax preparers; prospects for employment may be better in smaller cities or rural areas.

Although tax laws are constantly evolving and people look to tax preparers to save them time, money, and frustration, new tax programs and online resources are easing the process of preparing taxes, lessening the need for outside help. Information is available at the touch of a button on tax laws and regulations. Tax tips are readily available, as are online seminars and workshops.

The IRS currently offers taxpayers and businesses the option to "e-file," or electronically file their tax returns on the Internet. While some people may choose to do their own electronic filing, the majority of taxpayers will still rely on tax preparers— licensed by the IRS as electronic return originators—to handle their returns.

FOR MORE INFORMATION

For information on accreditation, contact
Accreditation Council for Accountancy and Taxation
1010 North Fairfax Street
Alexandria, VA 22314-1574
Tel: 888-289-7763
Email: info@acatcredentials.org
http://www.acatcredentials.org

For information on the certified tax preparer designation, contact
Institute of Tax Consultants
7500 212th SW, Suite 205
Edmonds, WA 98026-7641
Tel: 425-774-3521
http://taxprofessionals.homestead.com/welcome.html

For industry information, contact
National Association of Tax Consultants
PO Box 90276
Portland, OR 97290-0276
Tel: 800-745-6282
http://www.natctax.org

For information on educational programs, publications, and online membership, contact
National Association of Tax Professionals
720 Association Drive
Appleton, WI 54912-8002
Tel: 800-558-3402
Email: natp@natptax.com
http://www.natptax.com

For training programs, contact
H&R Block
http://www.hrblock.com

For information on becoming certified as an enrolled agent, visit
Internal Revenue Service
Department of the Treasury
http://www.irs.ustreas.gov

Index

Entries and page numbers in **bold** indicate major treatment of a topic.

A